# MOON 18 CITY

*WHOSE CITY? MOON'S CITY* **BY ESTEVAN TORRES**
**DIGITAL PHOTOGRAPHY.** 2017.

# MOON 18 CITY

MOON CITY REVIEW IS A PUBLICATION OF MOON CITY PRESS AT MISSOURI STATE UNIVERSITY AND IS DISTRIBUTED BY THE UNIVERSITY OF ARKANSAS PRESS. EXCHANGE SUBSCRIPTIONS WITH LITERARY MAGAZINES ARE ENCOURAGED. THE EDITORS OF MOON CITY REVIEW CONTRACT FIRST NORTH AMERICAN SERIAL RIGHTS, ALL RIGHTS REVERTING TO THE WRITERS UPON PUBLICATION. THE VIEWS EXPRESSED BY AUTHORS IN MOON CITY REVIEW DO NOT NECESSARILY REFLECT THE OPINIONS OF ITS EDITORS, MOON CITY PRESS, OR MISSOURI STATE UNIVERSITY.

ALL OTHER CORRESPONDENCE SHOULD BE SENT TO THE APPROPRIATE EDITOR, USING THE FOLLOWING INFORMATION:

MOON CITY REVIEW
DEPARTMENT OF ENGLISH
MISSOURI STATE UNIVERSITY
901 SOUTH NATIONAL AVENUE
SPRINGFIELD, MO 65807

SUBMISSIONS ARE CONSIDERED AT MOONCITYPRESS.SUBMITTABLE.COM.
FOR MORE INFORMATION, PLEASE CONSULT MOON-CITY-PRESS.COM.

ART DESIGN BY ESTEVAN TORRES
TEXT COPYEDITED BY KAREN CRAIGO

# STAFF

EDITOR MICHAEL CZYZNIEJEWSKI

POETRY EDITOR SARA BURGE NONFICTION EDITOR JOHN TURNER FICTION EDITOR JOEL COLTHARP ASSISTAN NONFICTION EDITOR JENNIFER MURVIN

ASSISTANT EDITORS EMILY S. ADERHOLD SHANNON ASHLEY ABIGAIL BENSON ANASTASIA BERKOVICH ANTHONY ISSAC BRADLEY NATALIE BYERS BRANDY CLARK SETH DOWLER HANNAH FARLEY BETH FISET LINDA FOSTER ALI GEREN EMILY GILLESPIE KATELYN GRISHAM KEVIN GRZYBOWSKI JOSHUA HENDERSON MARY HENN BRANDON HENRY SOON JONES EMILY JOSHU DANE LALE TAYMARIE LORENZO CHLOE MASSENGALE EMILY MCCORMICK WILLOW ONKEN KYLE OSREDKER SHANE PAGE ZACHARY RHEA NATHAN REAMES GENEVIEVE RICHARDS MICHAEL ROTHE BREEA SCHUTT GRACE SMITH REBECCA SPRAUER ESTEVAN TORRES TAYLOR VINSON ALEX WEBSTER KATIE WHITE SHANNON WICK ERIC YANDERS

ADVISORY EDITORS JAMES BAUMLIN W.D. BLACKMON LANETTE CADLE MARCUS CAFAGNA

# TOC

# GYPSY BEER
## MOTHS
ADRIANNE

My father brought gypsy moths to southwest Ohio. It was an accident. He brought firewood from my cousin's Rust Belt city, where nothing looked new and the gas station bathrooms smelled like aunts I hadn't seen in seven years. He was innocent, didn't know the stacks were infested with the most destructive pests of hardwood trees in North America. He ruins lots of things that way: by chance. The apple trees in the back yard, our black Lab's discipline, and my mother. It was never out of harm but malicious in the way that it was completely unnecessary. We never needed that much wood. Our fireplace burned twice a year. Angus already ate off the table, and my mother was fighting the urge to run, maybe even halfway gone by then.

The chaos that became our neighborhood after the infestation of gypsy moths was more than I thought possible. People cared about their basswood, birch, and sassafras. My next-door neighbor, who we called "the colonel," threatened to sue us. Two families moved across town because they were sure the moths would invade their homes. Photographers and environmental scientists swarmed our cul-de-sac. My mother's voice grew raw answering questions on the phone and extinguishing my worries of displacement. Our neighborhood was a petri dish holding fuzzy images of bacteria. We sat back and watched while dusty webs appeared on the branches around us. They were striking, if I didn't think about the wormy creatures building the soft, translucent nests, all the precious green leaves being nibbled on while we slept. Our no-outlet road became a corner in the back of a closet, covered in persistent cobwebs.

Like the flu, there is no cure for gypsy moths. No expensive spray that will wipe them out in ten hours. When people were less

concerned with killing trees, they set fire to acres of the infected branches. I wondered if that was the better choice about everything— to stop attempting fixes and just burn it all away. I dreamed about the smell of crisp ash leaving nothing left but pathetic trunks. Smoke crawling through the streets, making everything blurry. The sight of my mother's slate minivan disappearing behind the smog. She should have left when the cottonwoods in our front yard were seared down to bones, skeletons of their previous lives. My mother stayed, though, to guard what was left of our forests.

2

SAYLOR
GAGE **KERNELS**

An ex of mine returned from India, head shaved and claiming she'd found herself. She'd been riding a train, listening to *The Darjeeling Limited* soundtrack, reading Hemingway, when it all happened. The secret, she said, was to search your past for the most inconsequential event.

Is that yours, then? I asked. Her train ride to self-discovery was the most her thing she'd ever done.

She said no, claimed that *For sale: Baby shoes, never worn* is what triggered it all.

I thought of my brother then, a new father in a state prison. He used his weekly hour of computer time to browse sneakerhead sites for his son. *62% Under List Price: Baby Jordan VII's, Mint.*

No matter how I tried, my ex would not reveal her "kernel," as she called it, because she thought I'd mock her.

I asked if *that* could be my kernel.

Try again, she said.

I once caught my roommate and his girlfriend screwing in her car out behind the house. I triggered my car alarm to see someone else's shame.

No.

I'm always cold.

That means nothing, she said.

At the eighth grade dance I asked a kid with cystic fibrosis if he bought his suit at babyGap.

You were just a kid then, she said.

I told her I once went down on a girl because I was in love with her sister, a dancer in New York who would never make it.

Are you trying to hurt me? she asked.

I told her I just love a beautiful failure.

I had one for my sister, who played *The Office* theme song on marimba every day before marching band practice.

I had one for my mother who walked grocery store aisles for exercise.

I even had one for the clerk at the hardwood store who once told me "Until we have God-made machines, we're stuck with man-made ones" about a broken credit-card reader.

She asked, Why are you so afraid to find yourself?

I offered that I ate mashed potatoes with a spoon because I once poked my tongue on a fork prong and bled.

I offered that I checked behind the shower curtain whenever I used the bathroom, fearful of a phantom intruder.

I offered that the buzz of a lawnmower outside my window made me feel like I was never working hard enough to be who I was meant to become.

She agreed to tell me her kernel then, because I'd done such a poor job.

She took a shower after she'd shaved her head on a blistering July afternoon in India. She touched her bare scalp for the first time under that cold cold water and felt reborn. In that moment of rebirth, she saw a large black spider crawling the orange bathroom tiles and, without hesitation, crushed it against the wall. A godly power welled up in her then, like she was unstoppable, like she was Godzilla stomping through Tokyo. That's when she realized, she said, she wanted to be profound.

# STORMY SKIES CARDAMONE
## THOMAS ON THE GALACTIC FRONT

On a moving bus—from the hatch in the roof, through the emergency exit in the rear, out the Blue Bird glass windows—there are no forms of egress with which Han Solo is not familiar. You have saved him from mud puddles and snowbanks, dog yards and azalea gardens, and at the end of each rescue mission—your Princess Leia (your one and only mother): "Now, what is Han doing out here in Endor? How did he get stuck in the mud of Kashyyyk?"

"It was the Force, Princess," you'd say. "It was the Force."

That force's name was Danny, who was, like, as mean as a Sith lord and as handsome as a Hutt.

"If Han is so great, the Force will, like, totally save him." Danny does not understand how his thinking is completely peedunky.

You plead with Danny: "That's not how it works," you say. "Han can't use the Force!"

Clank. Clank. Clunk.

Those are the sounds Han makes as he bounces across the roof of the bus.

Lately, you are interested in stories of origin—for instance, how did Danny evolve into his present Danny-ness: Was he turned to the dark side or born into it? Think Darth Vader. Come back, Anakin!—but not so much that you ignore present and future scenarios.

When your own sense of the Force matures, you will stand up to the likes of Danny and shield the Princess from the cosmic reach of the Imperial Army. You will gather the younglings to you, saying, "It is all right. I will protect you from all that is base and poodoo." And knowing they are safe, they will say, "Wow, thanks!"

You feel these days cannot be far off.

☾

Saturday morning—cooking stromboli with Princess Leia, who has taken the day off of work so as to ensure that everything goes just right. On the calendar, "Russell's" is inked in big red letters.

"You fold the salami like this. You layer the cheese like this. The meat-to-cheese ration should be two to one," she says.

It is an endeavor more trying than Luke's training on planet Dagobah. You want to know why she simply doesn't order a large from Luigi's, as she normally does.

"You wouldn't just give Chewbacca the first laser blaster you found lying around, would you?" she says.

You love how she explains everything in ways you can understand, but you do not understand her attraction to Russell. "What if he is, like, a Jabba mercenary?" you say. You sulk and whine and hide in your room, refusing to come out, even when the Princess begs you to.

"Do you know how hard it is to be a single Rebel mom?" she says. "Do you think the Empire treats me with kid gloves?"

Eventually, you relent. Concessions are made—you will take your *Millennium Falcon* model to work on, out of sight—but not soon enough so as to not be late. As Princess Leia speeds aggressively down the road—mother of moons!—you wonder if she has been taking lessons from Han behind your back.

Arriving at Russell's, the car has barely stopped when she leaps from it and circles around back to pop open the trunk. A mechanical whoosh is followed by a piercing scream, and immediately you are stricken by panic: Was this a trap? (You knew it all along!) Would Darth Sidious stop at nothing to cripple the Rebel Alliance?

Joining Princess Leia, you find her staring down at the stromboli, crushed beneath a capsized *Millennium Falcon* and oozing marinara from either end: a ruptured and bloody intestinal tract. And you, too, feel crushed—by the weight of her downturned lips, by the arc of her shoulders, sagging and depressed. You want to say something, something like, "It is OK, the Force has not abandoned us," but before you can begin you are stopped by a raised hand.

"Don't," she says. "Not now." She turns to you, and in her eyes you see something you cannot recognize. "When I was your age," she says, "I wanted to be a national figure skater. I wanted to be Peggy

Fleming." But this is not the voice of the Princess. You have no idea whose voice this is, and suddenly you feel lost, so that when this voice says, "Let's go," and begins walking towards the house, you say, "Yes, mom," and leave the *Falcon* behind.

There are stormy skies on the galactic front as your mother knocks at the door. You are waiting with her under the eaves of Russell's blue-gray prefab when she leans down to you and whispers, "Do not despair, young padawan—at last, we have come to the planet Yavin. Here, we will be safe." And just then the door swings open, bathing the Princess in a pool of celestial light, and you cannot help but think, Yes, you are the one.

WENDY OLESON
# SUFFOCATE

I. It started at your shoulders, slick and spreading. Webbed fingers in satin gloves, the oil caressed and crept over your deltoids and dripped down your scapula. Scapulae, it seemed, were the point of no return. You pretended not to notice.

II. We'd stopped touching as much, our bodies grown softer and round: My belly pushed over my pants, and I didn't care who saw the strip of flesh where the T-shirt and waistband wouldn't meet. You kept covered. I'm working on it, you said, meaning the situation with the oil. You didn't have a car anymore, and I wouldn't admit to wanting one, even when the bus was bad.

III. By accident, that's how I'd found out. You'd been so careful with the laundry: Sunday morning, you hit the communal washers. When I'd wake at ten, the stacks of T-shirts and jeans, the towers of underwear and population of socks, would cover the coffee table. All of it clean. You couldn't do the sheets, though, because I was wrapped in them, and maybe you didn't think of them. You forgot about your pillowcase, and that's where the oil had seeped, glistening on the gray-blue flannel.

IV. I'd been healed by oil. I was a kid visiting Grandpa when the bug crawled into my ear. No need for a doctor in that Midwestern farm town. Grandpa poured the oil with shaking hands. And smiling. For every problem, a solution. The oil was warm with summer, thick with silence and, within a minute, stillness.

V. Remember the cigarette you dropped on the sidewalk of Los Feliz Boulevard, just east of Lowry? We remember it as a kind of last straw, and you remember the cop who saw, stopped his car, ran for you, sneered and spit and wrote that eight-hundred-dollar ticket complete with an appearance before the judge and community service picking up trash in Griffith Park. Your community service coordinator, Sam, dropped cigarettes from his truck despite Smokey's sign warning of *very high* fire danger. Sam talked about the sex he'd seen in the park and the couple that week who'd done it while a dog licked the dude's ear, really went at it, like there was food in there.

VI. The hole in my eardrum never healed. I hear it breathing at night: exhausted sighs and huffing. Air passing between my inner and middle ear. You hear it when you get close, put your ear to mine. It's funny when I get water in there: If I plug my nose and blow, it's like a cheap party horn tooting in a desperate new year. You agree.

VII. The oil has spread from the nape of your neck to Achilles' heel. You've hidden it from your family, our remaining friends. When under tremendous stress, some people hope to be hit by a car, but that car would glide right off you, as if you'd always had separate paths. I'd get hit on the ricochet because I'm home for bug or burden. A callus-pawed hamster working so hard on that wheel. But what's hard will soften and slip away.

VIII. The dead bug slipped out the next morning with fewer legs than it'd crawled in with. Relief, but not as much as the moment it stopped moving, fully seized by the oil. (Sometimes I think about that moment when I can't sleep at night, when my ear's breathing and my brain's crawling with fears, when I keep us both awake.) The earwig glistened on my pillow, and I yelled for Grandpa. *Got the fucker!* Grandpa whistled. We celebrated with fish sticks. My ear had secrets. Oily rainbows.

IX. Oil comes from compression: potential exuded, changed. I've never seen anyone compress dreams the way you do. Dreams bleed oil, and it's run through with rainbows. I imagine the

scene: One night soon, we're prostrate in bed with the oil in our mouths, choking on your promise and mine, those ideas to change the world turned to swirls and ripples of colored light. Justice and beauty coating our tongues and throats, making something, saving something, not ourselves.

# GARY PANICCROW

A study at a Midwestern college found that crows
　　could identify faces after a bunch of students
in rubber Dick Cheney masks harassed the campus murders
　　until the crows starting flying from anyone in said masks.
I laugh at the idea of a band of W. Bush's VP running
　　around an ivied quad throwing sticks and pebbles
at the cawing avians like the kids in *Lord of the Flies*
　　driving Piggy to his death, the crows not sure
where to go, black masses swerving this way and that
　　while knocking each other off their flight paths.
Think of the political theater: This was during their first term,
　　right before the GOP was reelected to the executive
branch. Somewhere—Missouri or Illinois—a branch sagged
　　under the weight of Dick-fearing crows. How, in crow-
caw-language, does one say "four more years" with sadness?
　　But then came another administration some swath
of the population hated as much as that one, but no Barack-
　　masked bird-molesters ruled our campus grounds.
Maybe we thought we'd grown. Until now, a hated president
　　again—who was the last one half of us didn't hate?
That last who didn't start a species into panic? Fill the skies
　　with beating, fleeing wings? The weather here today
is clear. Altogether elsewhere it isn't. Missiles to the sky
　　from ships far off a roiling country's coast. People run
into buildings like a line of ants, hoping it won't collapse
　　on them and burn.

1.

stink of his beers on Big Game day

gone-by springs of greasy TV chair
butts and ashes mounded in saucer
splayed buttonholes belly hairs framed

TV screen bodies pound against bodies
splayed buttonholes belly hairs
sunk in Big Game day

Big Game bodies pound against bodies
greasy head against chair sunk in Big
Game day butt mounded on gone-by springs

Big Game bodies drive against bodies
pile body on body

drive his body drive his mind

2.

shuts her nose to stink of Big Game beers
shuts her mind to greasy gone-by

# FIELD

shuts her eyes to TV screen
where bodies drive against bodies

opens her eyes to TV ad
Land Rover roving savanna-grass field

dreams ignition, start, drive
drive screaming in lane

her savanna-grass mind roving
brakes for Big Body

body against body

whole new field whole new field

EILEEN HENNESSY

BARBARA VARANKA
# AÑEJO

Tequila rings clean.
The cactus blossom:
both well cured
and curing.

How do they pull that rounded sharpness out?

Like a golden ring,
not bitter, not sour,
but haloed.

Hello, sweet friend.
You are gold tinted in the light.
You help me speak broken
Spanish to the cowboys.

14

# SPAGHETTI VARANKA
## BARBARA WESTERN

Oh, sandy-haired lamb, you were left bullet spurred
between the rusting tollbooths of a country highway

No one around. Your wounds stuffed red with silk.
The bullet blooms.

Once, you whipped a man round a screaming hydrant,
and rolled him into the gutter's watery rib.

Once, you pressed a thick brunette
against a door. Her weight sunk through her thighs.

You died in two-tone lace-ups. You died
on your way to the glittering desert,

the belly of the Holland Tunnel
lining up its hot-pink tubes in an endless plea to Maria.

# THIS SOUTHWORTH
## LUCAS NEIGHBORHOOD

The women across the street cackle, and we hear one say, "That irks the fuck outta me," and you call them witches because it's funny and it isn't, because it's insensitive but it's also a joke, so who cares. Right now, all but one of the women in the house are white; it's a white neighborhood, of course—it's always been, for as long as I've lived here—and though the area is getting hipper and cleaner and more expensive, these women still fit in OK, even when they get too loud. For some reason they've abandoned the front porch lately and they've started gathering near the street, on the steps, at dusk, some standing and some sitting as they smoke cigarettes, the smell and haze hanging over them before drifting down the block. You sometimes point out how they ignore us when we walk by; you sometimes point out how we can see into their house from ours, their bathroom window without curtains or shades or frosted glass, the light, when it's on, blazing crisp against the dark. You joke that, if we want, we could watch the women linger one by one as they get ready for bed, brushing their hair in front of the mirror, brushing their teeth, or looking, just looking. Sometimes I notice you staring in that direction as you close our bedroom shades at night, and then I notice you turn as if forcing yourself, and I see how much you want to glance back, to catch one more glimpse, but you don't, you don't let yourself, and I think you're good—or trying to be—and I wonder if it's for my benefit or for your own. Every morning at exactly 7:42, the women shuffle from the house to the bus stop at the end of the block, and every morning one of them straggles behind, running, speed-walking, having used the bathroom last, maybe, calling to the others to hold the bus, though nobody has that power in this city. We've lived in this

tiny house for a year now—we rent it—and it didn't take us long after we moved in together to realize that the house across from ours was a halfway house. In our year here, the women who've lived there, the women you call the witches, were the same for a while and then different and then different again. But their cackle and the shuffling toward the bus stop and the cigarettes, those didn't change, and neither did the woman who works there, the one who arrives at 7:23 every morning in her Buick and parks in front of our car or behind it and takes her slow time disentangling herself from her seat belt before crossing the street and climbing the stairs, purse dangling from her wrist as though it weighs ninety pounds. The woman who works there is black, and she has a laugh, too, but hers is louder, not a cackle; it's a deep laugh, a fine one, so fine it makes me think that exact phrase— "She's got a fine laugh"—though I've never used "fine" to describe anything, not even my day. Instead, when you ask how my day went, as you always do, I just say "good," as long as it was middle to a little worse, and if it was bad or really bad, I grunt or sigh, and if it was really, really awful, I just say "shitty." I don't like my job; I hate it, in fact. You don't know how many shitty days I have there, and I don't tell you because I hate the look you give when I do, your eyebrows, the way you ask if I need to talk or want a hug, and the way I have to tell you "no" because you're doting and making me feel as if you're forcing me to be happy, as if the fact that I'm not isn't my fault but yours, as if you might happily take on the blame for a bit of my unhappiness, your disappointment coming clear in your voice, the disdain, the way you believe happiness is a decision I can make, must make, and you can help if I just let you, though I'm not sure happiness means the same to us, and I'm not sure I believe it's even a decision worth making, anyway. We joke instead; we're always joking. At night, the women disappear inside; they use the bathroom and at some point the lights go out and the house goes quiet and we forget about them as they sleep. We watch a movie and drink a beer each—an expensive beer, an IPA, usually— and it's the same most nights because our days are long and we're tired. I sit beside you on the couch. I think about how the magnetism between us has become unpredictable, that there's no way to tell when we'll come together, no way to predict or force it. Sometimes at work, I think about buying a bottle of the cheapest whiskey and a two-liter of Coke like an old boyfriend of mine used to do. Whenever he

17

brought those things home, we knew what it meant, and I'd turn on the shittiest movie I could find, and we'd drink, really drink, until both plastic bottles were almost empty and the world was hazy, muzzy, the two of us caught in it, the alcohol leading us to the bedroom or not even letting us get there before we were naked on the couch and doing things we never did sober. I haven't tried this with you because I don't think you'd drink the whiskey, even with Coke; I think you'd just laugh a laugh worse than a cackle, a laugh with a "no" behind it, with a "That's ridiculous," with a "Why waste time doing something like that" and a "if we're going to drink why not good stuff" and an "If we're going to watch a movie, why not Kurosawa or Bergman or the great, great Bresson." And you're right—and I want you to be right—but I can't make love after watching Bergman or Bresson—I certainly can't fuck; those movies slow me, lock me in my own head, make me forget my skin. And I wonder if the women across the street, those women recovering from drugs or crime or abuse or maybe all three, if they can possibly be happier there, happier than I am here, and I tell myself no, no. I was a kid once, in this neighborhood; I knew those women—I heard them laughing, screaming through open windows in the summer. My mom warned me against them—the women down the block. They were always down the block. They used to look to me, somehow, like they were free, used to sound that way, and the neighborhood was full of them before people like you lived here, before people like you started moving in. So one night, as you turn on the television and run through the stack of movies you got from the library—movies in black and white, many with subtitles, many silent— and you ask me to choose, I suggest we turn off the TV instead and go up to our dark bedroom and open the shades, our shades, and watch, just watch, as the women across the street cycle through the last part of their evening, their only moment of silence and privacy. You say "no" as I thought you would—you laugh along the nerves of your tongue— you think I'm joking—and I don't blame you; we joke around a lot— we do it when we otherwise wouldn't be getting along—and for a second I want to laugh and say, "It was a joke; it was a joke so who cares,"—but I don't; I say, "I'm serious, it'll be good," and I take your hand and lead you up the stairs. You sit on the side of the bed, and I pull the shades all the way up on both windows and sit down next to you, our shoulders touching, barely. We watch and we don't laugh; we

don't make a sound. Across the street their bathroom light is on as always, and soon a woman appears, one of the older women living there now, maybe in her thirties, and, though we're too far away to see the drips of the water, we watch her wash her face and we watch her run her hands through her hair and study herself in a mirror we can't see and we watch her run her hands through her hair again. She leaves and a girl comes in—one of the youngest, maybe nineteen or twenty. The girl closes the door—we can just make out the edge of it—and from the angle of her shoulders we know she's happy to be alone. We watch her lean forward, crouching, kind of, and it looks as if she's sliding off her pants, and though we can only see her from her waist up, when she takes off her shirt, we assume she must be standing there naked. She stares into what we assume is the mirror for a minute that feels like ten and then turns to the window and stares through it as though she's searching for us, her breasts small and her arms impossibly thin and her hands—though we can't see them hanging below the edge of the window frame—shaking. I lean back like I'm dodging something. "She can't see us," you say, but your voice is all breath, all fear, even if I can't pinpoint what either of us are afraid of. The girl has tattoos over her upper arms and she has one where I have mine, on her left side just above her hip. She has, in fact, the same thing I do but a different image—the tattoo everyone in this neighborhood gets at some point—a dragon, a go-to—but hers is sleek and violent and maybe angry, and suddenly I want a cigarette, though I haven't smoked since I moved in with you. "We should turn on our light," I whisper as though the girl might hear. "We should let her know we're watching." But you don't do it and I don't either, and the girl continues to stare into the dark as though watching us watch her, and suddenly she starts to laugh, just for a second; then, just as suddenly, she turns like she's heard a knock, and she hurries to put her clothes on and glances out the window one more time and disappears, and the bathroom remains empty for another moment before the next woman comes in to use the sink and take her place.

# LOCAL GIRLS, VARELA
## GIOVANNA 2001

While waiting for our order at Burger King, Gigi and I leaned against the condiment stand with our hands in our pockets—posing for the Guess ad we pretended to live in—and watched four boys sitting in a booth, clutching Whoppers with dirty hands and dividing a chocolate milkshake into three courtesy cups. Bloody knuckles extended from their wrist casts like nerve endings dangling from toothless gums, their skateboards lying on the floor like overturned big rigs. Gigi and I put on our paper crowns and suicide-bombed our water bottles at the soda fountain. We wore butterfly tops and sparkly denim and shared onion rings on the walk to Gigi's house.

"I want a boyfriend with good genes and bad self-esteem," Gigi said. She liked this kid they called the Puerto Rican Paul Walker. His modified Eclipse had a blue underglow and dolphins airbrushed on the hood. Gigi and I got our horoscopes from the backs of Spanish tabloids, and girls at school traded us nail polish and hair clips for their love charts. The kid Gigi liked was a Capricorn and therefore resourceful and pessimistic and also my natural enemy.

I curled a baby snake around my wrist when we cut through the car wash parking lot. "Give him a kiss," I said. The snake stuck its tongue out when Gigi pecked its cheek. As we got closer to Gigi's house, I unwrapped the snake from my arm and wore it like an ankle monitor, hoping her parents wouldn't notice the latest in our collection of animals we'd bring home. Her dad and his friends were sitting on metal foldout chairs in the garage, and watching Ruiz vs. Holyfield on pay-per-view; her mother and the other wives played cards at the domino table. Next to them was a large cooler filled with Medalla cans and a two-liter Coco Rico, sprouting like ragweed from a pile of ice.

"It's a miracle," her mother said in Spanish, circling a Krazy Straw inside a glass of soda. "They came home empty handed."

Gigi's mom entered every cereal box sweepstakes and sold pyramid-scheme cosmetics at the weekend swap meet. She looked like those women in telenovelas who spend entire episodes posed dramatically on a chaise or under a chandelier while smoking cigarettes and crying in pageant dresses. One time, Gigi, her mother, and I walked into Claire's at the Florida Mall, right when a teenaged Claire's employee was about to pierce another teenaged girl's nose. She did a double-take as she pulled the trigger on the piercing gun. "Oh, my God," she said, looking at Gigi's mom. "I thought you were Daisy Fuentes." She looked back down at the girl's nose and realized she'd missed the mark. Her expression was like a lumberjack who chopped down the wrong tree.

Gigi and I were six years old and left Claire's that day with mood rings and a pair of necklaces—each one with a smiling turtle holding half a heart.

As we walked by the adults in the garage, I thought about the ice melting inside the cooler and how cute our snake would look in its own little swimming pool.

In the living room, Gigi's brother and his friends were playing Xbox and sharing a bag of mini-marshmallows. I moved three mostly empty cereal bowls to one corner of the coffee table while Gigi ran upstairs. She reappeared with a handful of Barbie clothes, and we sat on the couch dressing the snake in tiny poodle skirts and strapless gowns. We sent the snake down a runway on the coffee table, imitating things we'd imagined Cindy Crawford would say on *House of Style*. "The pink satin dress is impressive against this beauty's bright-yellow scales," Gigi said into her purple hairbrush. "Can you do that somewhere else?" her brother asked.

Gigi wanted to be a cowgirl for Halloween. I wanted to be Lady Godiva or Cher, "Because we have the same sun, moon, Venus, and rising signs," I said.

"You just wanna wear a really long wig, don't you?" said Gigi.

After school one day, we ran into the kid Gigi liked. We'd gone to the gas station where we always spent leftover lunch money on candy and slushies. He was filling the tank of his other car—a black '99 Toyota Celica—when he looked up to see Gigi and me leaving the store and passing a group of men who called to us—in the same

tone that every local girl in every gas station in every town, ever, had learned to walk faster from.

"Hey," said Gigi's crush in our general direction, holding the nozzle inside the tank. A thin breeze threw his shoulder-length hair around, exposing a scar on the left side of his neck and a tattoo of a dagger the size of a paper clip piercing through it. He looked like the grown-up version of those kids who starred in anti-drug videos they'd show us in DARE class. Big, sad eyes and puffy lips beneath an unusually pronounced philtrum. Simultaneously too serious and too vulnerable-looking to be 21.

Gigi and the group of men and I stopped and turned to look at him, none of us knowing who he'd referred to. Cruz Rodriguez stood there for a moment, looking shocked that anyone had turned around to listen. The ticker on the gas dispenser had stopped, the low gurgle of fuel lurching through the hose now silent.

"Shut up," he said, looking at the men.

Gigi and I sat on the floor of my room, watching what was left of the top-ten music video countdown. One of the frogs we'd brought home from the flea market two weeks earlier was creeping up the sides of its aquarium, its tiny footsteps sounding like water leaking from a tap. I poured my remaining gummy worms into my melted slushie and mixed it around with a plastic fork so I could eat it like spaghetti. Gigi searched my makeup bag for a tube of metallic-blue mascara. Both of our mood rings had turned a bright orange, and we hadn't stopped talking about Cruz since leaving the gas station.

"See? Not all Capricorns are trash," Gigi said, looking into my heart-shaped vanity mirror while applying the mascara.

The snake got pretty long and heavy by Halloween. Gigi dressed as Britney Spears and wore the snake around her neck all night.

Gigi was right about the wig. I wanted a long, bleached wig that would graze my ankles and drag behind me like a bright veil, glowing as it picked up pebbles and orange blossoms on the street. I wanted to flip it over my shoulders at the neighborhood pool, in front of all the boys wearing Jason masks and basketball shorts.

# ORANGE VARELA
## GIOVANNA WORLD

I met my boyfriend inside the Big Orange on Highway 192. He told me he was a sponsored skater—which I figured meant he was a dropout and probably a fugitive. I was an apprentice for an amateur tattoo artist and practiced by tattooing local vagrants who lived behind the water park. I'd give them bottles of Rolling Rock, and they'd let me vandalize their bodies with sticks and pokes, using sewing needles sterilized with Bic lighters. I drew lots of praying hands, lots of 407s that summer. He watched me try on a tank top with the Big Orange logo on it, and I pretended not to feel him eating me up.

"Sick shirt," he said, sitting on the floor inside the Orange.

"True," I said.

He looked like a miscarriage, and I liked his bleached hair and greasy eyelashes. We spent months inside that Orange, shooting darts through postcards and sucking pulp off each other's cuticles.

I let him bind me in rockweed at Cocoa Beach. He makes himself the size of an almond and squeezes into a valley between my ribs.

"I would die for you," he says, tightening ocean cables against my skin.

"That's nice," I say.

Far away, a dolphin cries out. Something about the traffic or other dolphins not minding their own goddamned business.

My boyfriend grew up in the same trailer park as this kid who was on *America's Most Wanted*. He showed me a picture of them at a birthday party when they were seven. They stood in a layer of trash on the bed of a pickup, shooting orange soda into each other's mouths from transparent water guns.

Near the end of summer, a picture of my boyfriend is posted on a billboard between the Gator Motel and a bowling alley. "You're

famous," I say. I sit in his lap and inhale the bleach from his scalp as he U-turns at the traffic light for hours.

Kingdom Hall leaves their flyers and booklets on my front step every Sunday morning. I never bother to take them inside and do something with them, like throw them away or use the illustrations to practice drawing Christ. So many have amassed on my welcome mat that my boyfriend and I go out there some nights and kiss on top of prayer cards.

After getting out of the shower tonight, I walk into my bedroom to find him under my mattress, chewing on peroxide bottle caps and clutching religious literature. He's lost his one and only sponsor— Blond Boy—and his roots are coming in dark and slick, like cuttlefish ink slowly corroding a layer of white gauze, so greasy it looks like celluloid. They've found out about his warrant, and that means the Orange County boys will be here soon. We spend the next two hours burning smiley faces into each other's necks and shoulders, first with cigarettes, then with switchblades glowing red-hot from a flame torch.

We sit on the floor, eating pancakes with cherry cream while acting out our visitations. I hold a fuzzy bedroom slipper to my ear and crocodile cry as he picks up a dish sponge for his pretend phone. He puts a hand up to the imaginary window and makes me promise to decorate my room with his suicidal love letters.

"Wallpaper the entire thing," he says, ashing a cigarette on my tongue.

"I will," I tell him and use one of the switchblades to carve my name into his knuckles.

Although he grew up eating citrus like drinking water, my boyfriend has an aversion to acid, and I can taste the blood from his split gums whenever we kiss after he's had orange juice or an entire grapefruit for breakfast. While he's sitting here letting me scar his fists, I try to picture how he'll look in one of those jumpsuits: his hair back to its natural brown, the skin on his fingertips rough and thicker than soft-serve. It's what happens when he gets sad and skins tangerines by the handful. I'm seeing it now, so clearly that it feels like a memory: a fresh set of cracked hands, another swollen mouth behind glass. "Lay off the acid," is what I should tell him but probably won't.

"You won't," he says, cutting off my hallucination.

"How do you know?" I ask. I'm startled and guilty. He never told me he reads minds.

"You'd wallpaper this room?" he asks, flinching from my blade opening his skin. "You won't even bring in the brochures from the Jehovah's Witnesses, and that's, like, God stuff. They even visit you every week."

# I HAVE FANTASIES ABOUT THE POST OFFICE WORKER ON 8TH ST.

MELISSA BOSTON

If I have any romantic notions left, please let me mail them
with stamps I will need to purchase. Don't offer me seasonal,
just Forever. Don't comment on my shabby tape job. I don't care
if the box stays together.
I prefer the romantic notions to scatter from your mail cart,
or the mail dock room, or fly through the mail truck's window
in a quick breeze until they trash someone's lawn.
Don't be kind and feel the need to tape my box and tell me
you've seen worse jobs and this is what you do for them.
These romantic notions don't deserve the gesture.
Let there be another conversation between us instead:
one about the accident that made you limp, or
how many blue shirts you own, or
how many six-packs and cheese sandwiches you downed
when the child support became too much, or
how you had to move in with your cousin and sell the dog.
Let us talk about driving to Paris to be the first to summit
Hog Jaw Mountain so we can be the first to send pictures
to peakery.com. and say *Sooie!* Let us find another town
after that one, a town with an unsubstantial Southern name—
Sweet Home, Sugar Grove—where we can get a room
and a bottle of Old Gran-Dad, where we can watch reruns
on a bedspread that is the color of urine, and where we can't
help ourselves intellectualize our needs but only press each other
into the worn, discolored mattress to distract us.

# TO BANG HIS HEAD AGAINST THE WALL

CHARLES HARPER WEBB

As a boy, he hung pinups of mountain goats
      above his bed. He idolized woodpeckers—
red-headed, downy, ivory-billed. At rock
      concerts, he'd bang his head against thin air,

hair flailing like a willow in a hurricane.
      The head-butt was his favorite wrestling finisher,
the buttees flipping like beached fish,
      consciousness *kerthunked* out of their skulls.

Grown now, he bangs his head into walls
      to show his wife and kids, *I care this much!*
*And this! And this!* He does it to warn,
      *If I hurt myself, don't doubt I can hurt you.*

He does it for philosophy: *I bang my head,*
      *therefore I am.* He does it for religion:
*See how I suffer for your sins*—and for art:
      *Who needs Shakespeare when you have me?*

He does for revenge: *tit* for *tat*, and *tat* for *tit*.
      It's in his genes: a bam! bam! bam! hammered
down through rageful centuries. "Life is hard,"
      he tells the doc. "But my head's up to it."

# ACROSS FROM A WOMAN TRYING TO READ <span style="font-size:smaller">REES</span> THE ORIGIN OF CONSCIOUSNESS IN THE BREAKDOWN OF THE BICAMERAL MIND ON THE C TRAIN

ELIZABETH

28

Taking his bagged bottle
from between his pants and gut,
he rolls back his head
and greedily swigs.
His sweat reeks with clout.

He cuts a fart and caws.
The man in a bad wig buries his nose,
batting Diane Arbus eyes.
That librarian type looks like
she's praying no one thinks it's *her*.

The thing is how public
transportation has become.
The young woman is trying to read.
She steadies herself on a pole
and impatiently flips a page.

Slowly, people stand,
shuffling center. Soon a clutch
huddles in one corner.

## ACROSS FROM A WOMAN TRYING TO READ THE ORIGIN OF CONSCIOUSNESS IN THE BREAKDOWN OF THE BICAMERAL MIND ON THE C TRAIN

The doors open and he waves
them off, blessing each one,

those who have never
enjoyed anything so much
as air, as breath.
He is the conductor.
This is their stop.

ELIZABETH REES

# WE THREE QUEENS

SHELBY DALE DEWEESE

We were standing at the bus stop, enough
sidewalk between us
to say I don't know you.
When the man in the truck idled,
hollered things we couldn't hear
but could taste, could feel like hair
on our tongues, we became a united front
of furtive glances. We became
sisters of the bus stop, sisters
of the early morning, of the commute.
We became sisters with our hands
in our pockets, on our whistles or our phones.
Our feet planted one step closer
to each other, our eyes on the truck and
not on the truck.

# SOMEPLACE TO BE
### A.R. ROBINS

I'm sitting on the sidewalk in front of Jimmy John's, smoking a cigarette and massaging my wet calves through the black cloth of my uniform slacks, thinking about Jack, my dealer. His house is just a couple blocks away from this Jimmy John's, but that's a couple blocks in the opposite direction from my apartment, and I'm not sure if I want to get high more than I want to be home, not sure if seeing him is worth the extra walk. I'm tired, my eyes heavy like two lead marbles, my calves sore from hours of standing. As I massage my legs, I can feel the heat waves from the sidewalk pushing softly against my ankles, as if the sidewalk itself is sighing into the cool night air, tired from its own long day of being walked on. I watch the light on the stiff pole in front of me. Moths meander around the buzzing yellow bulb, making mindless figure eights, their awkward movements sincere. I watch those moths until my eyes begin to water from the noise of that light.

I heard once that moths use the moon to migrate. They evolved to be attracted to light, and at night they follow the moon toward wherever it is they need to go. That's why they float around light bulbs, because they can't tell artificial light from moonlight. We really fucked moths over.

I begin stretching my legs in front of me, popping my toes inside my slick-resistant shoes, revolving my ankles.

(I'm unwinding, like string on my father's fishing pole, my body long and ready to be flung forward into something. I enjoyed fishing as a child. We fished for food, not for sport, but I still enjoyed the quiet respite of a day at the lake, when my father was not my father and I wasn't his daughter—we were

just the sound of the waves on the dock and the movement of our poles and the dragonflies that buzzed around us.)

I live two miles away from the CiCi's where I work, so walking home takes at least half an hour. I only make $6.50 an hour washing pizza pans, and a taxi is at least $7 dollars one way, so a ride home is more than an hour of work, after taxes. A taxi isn't worth it, especially if you consider that it isn't normal time I'm trading but work time, time in that black uniform that smells like sour milk no matter how many dryer sheets I use, time with my feet always wet and stinking and peeling, and time with Walter, the prep cook who works in the back with me. Walter likes to guess what color underwear I'm wearing every time he sees me because one time, when I bent over to pick up some dirty pans beneath the buffet, he saw that I was wearing red underwear, and I guess he couldn't get it out of his head.

"Black," he'd say when he saw me enter the kitchen. He rarely said anything else to me, just some color.

I sometimes call a cab in the mornings when I'm not broke so that I don't stink from sweat when I get to work, but I usually walk home at night to save money. I also walk home at night so I can figure out if I want to see Jack without having to ask the taxi driver to take me to see him. I don't know his address, just where he lives, so if I tell a taxi driver to take me to his place, I have to state where we are going street by street, and that feels bizarre, letting someone else in on what was going on between us, which isn't much. It's easier to walk the two miles at night, to step onto his porch and knock on his door four times to let him know I'm not a cop, to see him smile at me through the screen between us.

I take risks walking home, especially at night, though I usually see more shit to be scared of during the daytime. Like the time I saw a man strangling his girlfriend in his driveway. I was walking home one morning, only a few blocks away from my apartment, when I saw a couple fighting with each other. I wasn't scared, but I stopped walking when I saw them because I would have had to walk right in front of them both in order to get home, and I didn't want to be part of it in any way, not even as part of the scenery. I stood still, watching them scream at each other, him calling her "bitch," her screaming "bitch" back. Then he grabbed her by the throat with one arm and pushed her down on the hood of the car in their driveway. That surprised me

because they were about the same size, both big football-player types with broad shoulders and thick legs. It didn't seem like he would have been able to take her down so quickly, but, then again, she probably let him do it.

(That's how you have to handle it; when you watch something come at you, you just have to fold into it. Once, on a fishing trip with my father, I watched a dragonfly fly into my eye. I didn't flinch, just watched it smack into my pupil. I pulled its legs out from under my eyelids while my father laughed, and then I cradled my eye just the way you cradle your eye after someone hits you in the face. It wasn't like I wanted the dragonfly to crash into me; it's just that I wasn't afraid.)

The girl got away. He stopped choking her after a few seconds, probably because he realized she was going to just let him do it. That's the best strategy when someone is hitting the shit out of you or choking you. Usually, they're too chicken to kill you, and if they aren't, they were going to kill you anyway. Some girls fight it, but there's no point.

I've been living in this house with five bedrooms, where this guy, Eric, rents out rooms to college students. I'm not in college. I dropped out about a year before I moved in, but, for some reason, Eric lets me rent out the room. Jack doesn't like that I live there because he thinks Eric wants to sleep with me, but he knows I don't have a choice because I can't pass a credit check, and Eric doesn't even make you sign anything.

Besides, Jack doesn't want me to move in with him, says I'll run him out of business. Maybe Eric does want to sleep with me, but he never tries anything like that. Not yet. I know that if it happens, he won't think about it first; he'll just find himself doing it. I don't look or act like one of those girls that men think about hooking up with. Men just hook up with me. They never think about it. I won't move out of Eric's setup until Jack tells me I can move in. I have it pretty good there. One month, I couldn't make rent because I was working fewer hours and I'd spent all my money at Jack's, so Eric let me live with him for free a few months so long as I took care of his dogs while he went on some trip for his job to wherever the fuck.

They are terrible dogs, but that isn't their fault. Eric works in an office, a real nine-to-five kind of thing, and he keeps those dogs in these little cages in the basement while he's at work. They're too big, too full of energy to be left in cages. They need to run around and just get rid of everything that's inside them, but he never thinks about it like that. I tried walking them when he was gone on his trip, but they were too strong for me, so I usually gave up and just let them run around the neighborhood for a few hours. I'd smoke a bowl, take a nap, and then go looking for them after I woke up. I usually found them behind this Jimmy John's because some kid started leaving lunch meat in the back for them like they were strays.

(I was waiting for my father to pick me up at the bus stop. I stood a few feet away from some boys on my bus route because they said I smelled bad, and maybe I did. There was a puppy with a black face and a red collar. It belonged to somebody, but no one knew what dogs belonged to anyone in that town because they all just roamed free in the dust. The boys picked the puppy up, and I didn't see what they did to it because I wasn't looking at them directly. I never made deliberate eye contact with them; that was just asking for trouble. I didn't see what they did to that puppy, but I heard it. Then I watched it walk away from us like it was already dead.)

If I go home, Eric might be up, and maybe he'd try talking to me about films I've never seen or records I've never listened to. Maybe he'd make fun of me for getting too high last night and falling asleep in the living room with puke on my lips. Maybe, while he talked, his eyes would fall on the crotch of my pajama shorts, and I'd have to pretend like I didn't notice. Maybe he wouldn't be home, and I'd be able to catch something on TCM, something old and simple and clean.

I'm stretching out my legs on the sidewalk. I'm trying to decide, and I can smell myself. I smell the way a girl smells when her old shoes are soaked in dishwater, when her body has been sweating over hours of old sweat, when her tampon has soaked through to her underwear, when her hair hasn't been washed for a few days, when she has smoked a few too many cigarettes. If I see Jack, he'd smell me, and maybe I wanted him to. Jack liked to work on cars. Says cars are the only art. Sometimes, he will come to Eric's to pick me up, and he'd usually smell

like armpit and WD-40, and that bitter chemical smell makes me shiver sometimes, makes me want to bite into him like he's a leather strap.

A man in a red Ford Ranger pulls up in front of me.

"Are you lost?" he asks me, his eyes squinting like the light on the pole above us is blinding him.

"Nah, man. I'm just waiting for my boyfriend to pick me up."

"You need some spending money?" he laughs.

(I watched my father cut scales off a catfish while it was still alive, sucking up the dry air on the dock with a knife running over it over and over again. I stopped fishing after that. I figured I was hurting the fish from the very beginning, figured the hooks weren't good for their mouths and throats, figured the air burned into them like so many more hooks, but I always assumed the pain was necessary. I understood the reason for pain. I understood the long bodies of deer that looked like Bambi that would sometimes dangle from a tree behind our trailer. I understood the trembling rabbit in my father's arms after he would break its neck. The fish swallowed hooks because it was better for us to eat fish in the summer than to eat canned meat. It was fair. I absolutely understood the fairness of one creature's pain for the benefit of another, but it seemed like too much then. Watching him scale the fish with its eyes open and its body heaving for air, its mouth like a woman screaming, it felt like too much cruelty. It wasn't worth the enjoyment I got from catching it; it didn't seem like a fair trade.)

The guy in the Ranger drives away, and I'm out of cigarettes. There's a gas station still open a few blocks in front of me. I'm backtracking, but it's worth the walk, I guess. The cigarettes are more expensive there, but it's not like I can go someplace cheaper. While I'm walking I'm noticing some dandelions between the cracks in the sidewalk because I have a habit of looking down wherever I go.

(My father always made me tell him how to get home after we took a trip because he thought it would teach me how to have a sense of direction. Every time we'd come to a fork or a four-way, he'd ask me which way to go, and I'd choose without

thinking, and he'd drive wherever I told him to drive without letting on that I'd chosen right or wrong. All those country roads looked the same to me: same signs, same trees, same wildflowers in the summer, same gray snow in the winter. After a few hours of driving, he'd give up and just stop asking me questions, and we'd be home late. As far as I knew, every choice I made on those drives was the wrong one. I never knew the way home no matter where we were coming from.)

Dandelions used to be my favorite flower until I found out they were weeds. That sort of made me feel dumb, like I was too stupid to know the good flowers from the bad ones, like when someone buys you top-shelf vodka but you prefer the cheap stuff. There are people out there with a taste for what's good, and there are more people out there deciding what's good, and I've always wondered how it is anyone can tell.

I still kind of like dandelions. I like how dandelions peek out between the cracks in the sidewalk, like they can just feel the sunlight when they're buried in cement, and they just know that if they take this turn and that turn somewhere, they'll find the light and be able to breathe. I like how messy they grow in the sidewalks, like when you don't shave enough around your bikini line. I like how when they're dying, they just turn into something you can make a wish with.

The light around this gas station likes to hum at you. It's heavy, like the light is a fog you have to slice yourself into. I feel like I'm floating in it, like my body is made of whatever that light is made of, and I'm just blending into the air like a beam from a flashlight. I think I remember a teacher telling me once that beams in a flashlight move on for eternity, that they make a line that just goes on forever, and that all lines go on forever in theory, and I don't really remember the point of the lesson. I just know that I really liked thinking about the lines that drift away from a flashlight into space, moving and moving. I still feel peaceful thinking about it.

I see a woman in front of the gas station door, wobbling around a little, swinging her arms up and down around her like a penguin, I guess. She looks kind of rough, wearing sweatpants that don't fit, maybe never did, her hair wrapped in a dirty scarf. Her gray T-shirt has a picture of Tweety Bird on it, but one of his legs has peeled away. When she sees me, she looks directly in my face like she knows me.

"Hey, girl!" she yells, her voice muffled softly by the light around us. "Hey," I answer.

She walks up to me, taking these long steps like she's stepping over something, like she's got some stepping-stones in front of her. Her body is bouncing to a different rhythm than her legs, and I'm wondering how she's keeping balance.

"Hey, girl. Hey, girl. So hey, girl. Listen, girl, my car broke down just up the street, and I'm just trying to get some cash to use a pay phone. I just need some cash, whatever you got."

"That's some shit," I say, then I pull out some change from my pocket, just a few quarters and some smaller stuff. Her hand touches mine as I'm dropping the change, seamless, like there wasn't ever any distance between us before. She smiles.

"God bless you," she says, and then she starts wobbling around again, moving away from me toward the other end of the sidewalk in front of the gas station. She starts jumping around a little, like a boxer, like she's got too much in her legs to keep her standing still. I don't bother her. I'm already feeling guilty about giving her change.

(My father and I were pulling weeds around the front porch of our trailer, weeds taller than the leaning porch in front. We were throwing them around on either side of us, like we were rowing in a canoe. My father was working closer to the porch, and he cleared away this section around the stairs and found a web with a large spider in the center, black and blue. I'd never seen a spider so blue, like a blue I'd only ever seen in picture-books about the ocean, and that web was glimmering all silver and white. The web was round and symmetrical, like the way someone might draw a spiderweb. I stopped working so I could get a better look at the spider on that perfect web, and I remember the fear in my feet and hands, warm and opaque. I felt connected to the ground with the heavy fear of seeing something so beautiful that you can't make yourself understand it, you just keep your distance and watch. I didn't see my father get a bottle of lighter fluid, but I watched him douse that blue spider with it, and I remember the way it jumped, like if a jump were a scream, that's how it jumped, and I felt like screaming too.)

The light inside the gas station sort of bounces off the white tiles in the floor, a more evened-out and sterile light, and my eyes are having trouble adjusting. I walk around the aisles a little because I need some tampons, but I don't know why I'm even bothering because I can only afford cigarettes and maybe a large soda. I don't find any tampons. They're probably closer to the front counter, maybe to keep people like me from shop-lifting them.

There's a bathroom in the back, so I walk in and pull down my pants and try to assess my situation. My thighs are saturated with blood, some of it dried and brick-brown around the edge. There are no paper towels, so I take a wad of toilet paper and wet it in the sink and start wiping around my legs and crotch. My underwear is wet with thick blood, so I pull them off and take them to the sink and carefully rinse the crotch, squeezing out the cloth until the water comes clean. I dry them in the hand dryer, but I'm too impatient to wait until they are completely dry, so when I put them back on, they are warm and moist and itchy.

I wash my hands and then take another wad of toilet paper and tuck it between my legs. I can feel the toilet paper there getting softer from the moisture. When I'm done, I walk around the bathroom a little to see if I dripped anywhere when I didn't have any pants or underwear on. I don't find any wet blood on the floor, but I see a streak of dried blood on the toilet seat, long and thin, like a cut with a razor blade. I know it isn't my blood, and maybe it isn't blood at all, but I wipe it away with another wad of wet toilet paper.

I walk up to the front counter, holding on to the wad of ones in my pocket. I'm remembering every moment between now and the last time I bought cigarettes, and I'm hoping that no stray ones fell out of my pocket when I sat down or stood up or pulled off my pants because I really would like to have some cigarettes of my own tonight. I don't feel like asking Eric or Jack for any.

"Liggett Menthol, please." My other hand is in my pocket with my ID, but he doesn't ask for it.

"You didn't give that bitch money, did you?" the cashier, a small man in a red cap, asks me as he looks for my cigarettes. I shrug my shoulders, and he shakes his head and smiles at me like he's never seen anyone so naive.

"She's been hanging around here all day. I'm about to call the police." I'm watching him look for my cigarettes, but he's floundering.

"They're on the bottom shelf. They're white with green stripes."

He grabs them finally and starts typing into his register.

"What'd she say to you?"

"Who?"

"That bitch outside."

"She said her car broke down."

His face flushes, and he starts shaking his head, and I'm holding out my wad of ones even though he hasn't told me the price yet.

"That's a crock of shit. So she comes in here and asks for the phone, but I don't want her making any long-distance calls, so I tell her she has to buy something. So then she goes to the bathroom, and she's in there for hours. Then she starts walking around my parking lot outside, scaring my customers, and a group of ladies comes in to use the bathroom and they're like, 'That bathroom is disgusting,' and I'm like, 'I just cleaned it.' So I walk in there and there's blood and shit all over the toilet and floor, and I know that bitch did it, so I go outside and tell her she needs to leave or I'm calling the cops, and she starts screaming at me about public property, which is a load of shit because this is private property."

I'm still holding out my ones, and he finally takes them from me.

"I think she gave herself an abortion in there. I've never seen so much blood. I swear to God."

"Maybe she had a miscarriage," I say.

"Maybe. I just fucking cleaned those bathrooms."

He gives me back my change, and some pennies fall on the floor. I don't pick them up. I just walk out into the parking lot, light a cigarette, and let my eyes adjust to the humming glow of the parking lot. The woman is watching me again, but she's on the other side of the parking lot, meandering around sort of irregularly. Then she wanders toward me like a moth, her arms out beside her kind of limp and awkward.

"Hey, girl. Hey, girl. So hey, girl. Listen, girl, I could really use a cigarette. You got any?"

I hand her three cigarettes, then I light another and give her that one too. I want to stand in the parking lot a little longer because I still have a long walk ahead of me and I don't feel like going anywhere, but this woman is watching me, not looking at me, but watching me like she's waiting for something. I start walking, dragging my cigarette and breathing out smoke, listening to that hum in the light, a hum like an awkward child. The woman yells out to me.

"Hey, girl. Where you going?"

"I got someplace to be," I shout back.

"Yeah, me too, girl. We all got someplace to be. I'm going someplace too."

I don't know what to say to her, so I leave her there to wander around in that parking lot with the moths and Junebugs. Her words are wiggling around in my head by the time I get back to the Jimmy John's. *We all got someplace to be.* It's stuck in there like a jingle. *I'm going someplace, too.*

# A DOG'S TAIL

*for Tatum: Baker St., Bakersfield, California (1980)*

## 1.

anger is a black emotion,
a depression that lives & feeds upon itself;
says so in Webster's third edition—
under *nigger*.

there's nothing effervescent
about anger
but its singular ability to get a rise out of others.

## 2.

across the tracks, in the blight of downtown decay,
5-0 mob four deep, an afterthought seeping malice.
they come flashing lights & sirens screeching to a halt,
a jagged blue line in the sand, a street gang
of paramilitary force:

those who sow misfortune & build mountains of ice.

## 3.

status quo in Milk & Honeyland: protect & serve
with extreme prejudice, a traditional bigotry
dividing black & white      rich & poor
to have & have naught.

4.

under the bridge Tatum guards his shopping cart,
crammed stem to stern with all he owns:
a top-heavy impasse that sows confrontation.

but dignity whispers syllables of struggle
into the ear of the downtrodden:

*stand & be counted, or kneel & serve*

like a prayer to the portrait of a cow
looking to be a tiger.

# A QUESTION FOR THE SPIDER

JACKI RIGONI

I want to sever every tie,
every dollar, toaster,
and down pillow that held your head
before it whispered your absence each night.

I want to release the red balloon
from grasping me to your circus,
but there are these strings attached
called our children.

How to hold them and let go
of you is a question for the spider,
who spins her own silk, stalwart,
transparent, and takes it down each night.
Some say she eats it.

# SAYS WHEELER
## LESLEY THE CAB DRIVER
## OF THE APOCALYPSE

For protection against zombie hordes
you want a woman who's fed up with
bleeding, whose flint-spark eyes irradiate
your bone-strewn caves while she fixes
you a peanut-butter sandwich. It's not
about skinny or baskets of decorative
gourds, not anymore, though famine
will harden her, though absence will
carve channels where once was pillow.
Much less about ammo and dominance.
Screw, or don't, the shaky sheriff who tries
not to be dickish. To hell with metabolic
yelling and facial scruff. You want—
hold on, these are slow, I'll just veer round
like so—you want a woman who knows
what the moon really thinks of you, says
well it's red, reflecting all our sunsets
or some such shit, now hurry let's move.

CLAYTON KROLLMAN

# HIEROPHANTS

There's been a rule against meeting in places with fluorescent lights (the literature is clear: Spirits and ghosts of all kinds are attracted to the flickering of old neon and mercury) since Genevieve had her breakdown. Genevieve had started coming when we were still in the basement of the church that let us use their tables for donuts and our big urns of coffee that take two of us to lift. Her thing about the lights got worse when her kid died. She started keeping a composition notebook documenting all the streetlamps that went out as she walked under them and always had it open trying to unpuzzle the Morse-based communiqués of somebody she called Junebug. We aren't a grief-consolation group, at least not technically, so the mothers among us withheld all advice, even as Genevieve started coming to meetings so drunk she needed to cover one eye to read the room number. Eventually, she stumbled into a roller rink trying to get to the dentist and the strobe light punctured something way inside and she sat down hard enough to crack her tailbone on the linoleum and wouldn't talk when the paramedics arrived or later at the hospital, to me, once I'd found out she'd switched me to her emergency contact since the split with her husband. I don't really want to know how she'd gotten my last name.

Another rule is no judgment. There was a guy who gave us a different name every time he introduced himself, who insisted there was a haunted vending machine on the floor above his ad agency's that would feed him prime info about the ancient Mayan civilization's disappearance in exchange for something he called "death coupons." When we responded with the typical mantras of solidarity, he waved his arms and warned us: The world is ending this year, and I'm the only one who knows because you people won't listen.

45

☾

The doctor is young, and I can see him eyeing my finger for a ring as he updates me on Genevieve's condition: idiopathic catatonia. I've heard it before, but I let him explain what they've done or want to do. With the way he talks I can't tell which it is. He makes a joke about how idiopathy is a fancy way of saying "we don't know why," air quotes and all. I've heard that before, too. I move my left hand on top of my right so he can see the wedding band with the teeth marks and then he's all business. He starts calling me ma'am and leaves right after checking Genevieve's eyes with a flashlight.

Genevieve and I sit looking at each other, if you can call it that, and I start in with the updates while the old television snows and hisses in the corner.

"There's a new kid that comes now. He spoke for the first time on Wednesday. Today's Saturday, I don't know if you know. I think you'd like him."

There are a lot of pauses with this type of talking. The conversation doesn't necessarily follow a narrative. I turn the wedding band around my finger to examine the little dents in the gold. That's all that's left. I've always had a thing about teeth—doesn't everybody? The movie we went to see on our first date was an old Korean flick where a jilted lover uses the little notch in the back end of a hammer to twist her clumsy unfaithful's teeth until the whole head's just pain and dental gore. He asked me if I had ever been with another woman.

"We went to a psychic on our honeymoon. We've always been interested, you see, and the ad online mentioned a specialty in couples. She had a little shack right on the Adriatic that made you understand why they're called 'Venetian blinds.' Because of the high rate of American tourism, she only did readings between three and eleven p.m. This also explained the unusually high lamp density, as she gave readings well into the unlit ocean night. We each wanted our respective tarot done and agreed to the price. When she explained the rules to us, total and utter acquiescence to the presence that might appear et al., we agreed to that too and swore on the two tarot decks like they were Bibles."

I laid on the bed next to hers and turned on my side to face her. I thought about telling her that I know I'm being overly sentimental, but wouldn't you be, too, when you talk to somebody like Genevieve?

46

"I didn't know their names then, but my husband had the Rider-Waite tarot pack and I had the much-less-commonly used Etteilla. We cut our respective decks. Mine shocked me and I took note that the thick carpet was probably designed specifically for that. Madame Flora took one of her veils and put it over her head, which gave me enough of a peek to see her raise an eyebrow. She first drew from my stack of cards: the Hierophant. She said something about either the person or process by which we make human holiness divine and guessed that we were newlyweds (I'm mostly paraphrasing), plus also alluded to some future infidelity. On whose part, she remained unsure—would I love to see her again and tell her all, but I know I'll never go back. I think she used the word 'transmute' and I rolled my eyes. Then, my husband's: the Hierophant, reversed. Up went another veil and her eyebrows, followed by the classic 'You Are In Grave Danger' bit. By this point I'm absolutely convinced that we're being scammed. Then, another Hierophant from my deck but clearly belonging to a different deck. Normally, I would laugh about something like this, yet the mood had shifted and I found myself almost hypnotized. When she asked for my husband's ring, he handed it to her, and I did not object when she brought it to her lips and bit down. Now hers, she told him. He didn't take it off my finger. I still remember how careful, how electric. She wouldn't accept payment but wished us luck and sent us on our way with just the five imprints from her teeth.

"The air did get cold, we both agreed afterward. I offered up: It could've been the A/C on a timer to sort of subconsciously heighten our sense of foreboding. That couldn't be less a possibility than meeting an actual seer. Although, if she were grifting us, why wouldn't she have demanded money?"

I showed Genevieve the marks, or at least I thought I did. I put it between her eyes and the static on TV. I held it out to where she was staring, is what I'm saying.

This time, it's all true, but it doesn't matter. She's the only person you can tell the things nobody else would believe, so you tell it all and tell it anyway; like talking to a plant to make it grow, eventually, you make up stories to have something to say.

The new ones at meetings are always too afraid to go for the free food. In fact, nobody really speaks their first time if they're here to take it seriously. I've been here long enough to hear almost everybody's first

47

CLAYTON KROLLMAN

time, and I remember the man speaking now. He's lost weight, so now the folding chair seems too big for him. I imagine I look the same, like a child who can't reach the floor. He's telling us the same story as always, which usually gets a tepid laugh from the newcomers at the end, even though the people that wind up here are generally pretty serious about the whole thing.

His wife had a ghost. They moved from one cheap studio apartment downtown to a different cheap studio apartment downtown, and she started noticing the dishes would be done when she got home from work, or her favorite necklace she lost on a cruise some prior June had appeared on the bed arranged in a heart, or she started finding little intricately folded dollar bills shaped like animals, etc. It's cute and harmless and seems the opposite of what you might expect from a ghost. Zero malevolence. So she confronts her husband, even thanks him. In the beginning the wife doesn't believe the man when he tells her it's not him, it's really not him, so she sets up this camera in secret, thinking she'll catch him being sweet. Now everybody's expecting him to reveal the twist where she sees an eerie blue glow doing something sinister like setting the table or adjusting the thermostat, but he just stops talking.

It takes him a second, still, to confess the affair; call it genuine remorse/shame/gravity. I still pity the wife. To expect one thing and watch the man you love with some stranger he met at a bar or somewhere worse.

So the wife leaves him. Gets away from the apartment, too, which leaves the ghost (who was pretty obviously and madly in love with this woman) alone with the man in an apartment where the couch is also the bed is also the dining room. Pretty soon he can't find his shoes, which is funny because he can see the whole apartment at once. The power bill goes up, except he's positive all the lights were off this morning. He's always cold. Then, one day, he sneezes, and in the aerosolized particles a figure resolves and, get this, flips him the bird!

"Genevieve, did I ever tell you about Betsy the giraffe who got struck by lightning at Disneyworld in front of all those kids? They say the smell was worse than the sound because it lingered. How about all the shoes underneath what's left of the Titanic? That no one knows why the fish haven't eaten through all that leather by now—if they can't or won't. Or that dog the Russians shot into space without an exit

strategy, Laika. Still up there. Do things rot in orbit? Animals are more in tune to the paranormal, everybody knows.

"There's a young woman you might remember from before, who used to come pretty often. The one whose mother had that dream about her father, where he wanted a tomato sandwich. It was so vivid that she didn't remember he was dead, and when she woke up to give him what he wanted, she even threw in a glass of milk for good measure. So the daughter opens up the fridge to find the plate with an index card and her dead father's name Sharpied in block letters. These days, when she shows up, she swears she saw her dog sitting on the couch in the exact same place her dad made a human-shaped depression in the cushion (from all those accumulated hours in front of the tube), which would be normal except the dog is flipping channels with the remote at a steady and purposeful pace before settling on an old PGA tournament where her father's favorite player does just fine."

I stop talking when Genevieve's ex-husband walks in with the doctor. Even though she isn't really there, we pretend she is. He at least greets me first. Genevieve didn't make me her medical proxy alongside her emergency contact, thank god, so I don't have to talk to the doctor again. It's the same one as before. He's had enough time for a haircut and looks even younger. I stand outside and try not to eavesdrop.

When her ex-husband comes out I tell him he looks thin. He says I sound like a mother, and then he corrects himself. You sound like my mother. His laugh is as empty as usual.

Like always, he thanks me for waiting then takes me to their house—his house now, I suppose—and we get it out of our system. Afterward, I stand at the mirror where I imagine Genevieve used to stand and reapply my makeup. Examine the bite mark on my neck and the finger-shaped bruises on my hips. He straightens his tie and says what he's supposed to say, as if we're characters in some film. If he feeds me one more cliché I'm calling it quits. That's how this works: You invent little conditions to make yourself feel better. Do I want you to know I understand it's wrong? I think we both know the answer to that.

He drops me back off at the hospital and kisses me goodbye. I remind him he's the one who told me not to have illusions about this, and he smiles without his eyes. I think of the word "wry," then "magnetic."

It's a personal game to head like I'm going to my car until he's out of sight. There's a quiet thrill to subterfuge. I sneak my way back up to Genevieve's room. She's sleeping as if she hasn't turned everything upside down. As if the meetings still help me now that I spend all my time here. I feel like taking her by her narrow shoulders and yelling in her face. I feel like curling up next to her and going radio silent along with her. Instead, I find the composition notebook she had on her when she was admitted and look through it. The illegible last page from the roller rink almost all black from the frantic overlapping of text in some misguided effort to make the chaos count. Then I just sit in the chair and try to sleep.

The thin morning light slants in through the window, and someone smacks the top of the television to get it to work like they do in movies. By now, the nurses know to wake me up. Besides, I'm always out of their hair before I'm any trouble. This time is different; I don't know why. Maybe I was feeling extra sentimental, or I'd forgotten one more thing about my husband. Maybe I just wanted to give it another shot. So I linger. When it's just the two of us, I try Genevieve again.

"Genevieve? I had this dream that the world was getting brighter and brighter and it works its way into your brain and hurts until it kills you. What's worse is even though the doctors know exactly what's wrong, they can't do anything at all except watch you waste away like you're starving, but they can't give you anything and—look—I'm still shaking. How can you be afraid of something you know isn't true? And I used to have another dream sometimes where I can't open my eyes all the way and there's this soft black thing that floats three feet away from me always and follows me to work and just bobs up and down in the air above my bed, never saying anything, and I never feel judged until I realize it starts getting closer to me in that sort of dream montage where time passes as a linear-but-not-quite-linear series of moments stacked up against each other where every night this thing (which I can tell is a figure now) hovers closer and closer until her long black hair makes contact and I wake up retching with, I swear to god, a bruise on my cheek where the hair touched down. Then there's that guy who used to come to the meetings who turned out to be famous—the magician who had a million-dollar reward for anybody who could prove the existence of anything supernatural. Did he miss the point or what? And whatever happened to him? He had a million bucks

on the line and barely listened. Was he a magician? I can't remember now. I know you do. Genevieve, please. He had that big white beard? He said something about starting a television show to expose frauds. Why wouldn't he help us? The meetings are different now. People are splitting off. You were there more often. Do you remember anything that could help?"

Speaking right now is a man built like a bulldozer, gripping the sides of the podium hard enough I'm surprised there aren't finger-shaped dents when he lets go. He tells us of the kinship he feels when he's turning left at an intersection and his car's blinker lines up with another car's. He thinks it's the only time he's fallen in love. We're not supposed to, but we think he's being a little dramatic. Most of us have been in love, or else why would we be here? He also tells us about the Dyatlov Pass incident, as if we didn't all spend hours and hours looking into it ourselves, and even hypothesizes aloud about what happened to the research team that went missing there. Did you know they found one of them hundreds of feet away from camp, dead from brain damage but without head injury? Neither did he, so you can appreciate our frustration.

Now there's a man who has just begun growing into his acne scars and is totally convinced the voicemails from his fiancé have changed since she died (from what I gathered, she went running on a beach with her headphones in and didn't hear the plane overhead make an emergency landing or explode seconds after the pilot escaped to safety or the propeller whizzing through the air and then through her). He says he remembers her telling him goodbye over the phone, but now, when he goes back and listens, she says she loves him first. Sometimes she apologizes, too. A few of us start to have trouble swallowing when he tries to say her name and can't. But then, as he cries up there facing us, something shifts in the group. No one wants to tell him he's making it up, whether he knows it or not, but we all think it meanly to ourselves. It isn't fair, we think, that he gets some sort of solace from beyond while we're stuck actually processing our grief, if you can call it that. Genevieve would've eaten this guy for breakfast. All of a sudden we can't wait for him to stop making such a spectacle of it all. Somebody probably mutters that they weren't even married. Our affirmations aren't as loud or enthusiastic as they usually are when he finally slumps back into his folding chair.

And now there's a teenaged boy who looks genuinely wigged out who asks if we can help him. He says he spends a lot of time on the Internet. He uses the word chagrin and pronounces it wrong, that's how young he is. Online, he's been chatting with a man who claims to come from the future, who says this is the year it all goes wrong. Oh, boy. Tell us something we don't know. According to this stranger, there's some outbreak of prions that can, against all odds, be transmitted genetically—lying dormant until almost a hundred years down the proverbial line. Anybody who eats beef this year is damning their offspring later on. Mad cow disease is the affliction du jour, but the man says he doesn't know what will happen now that he's made Contact. When the kid quotes this guy, you can tell which words are supposed to be capitalized. Eventually, the prion disease aerosolizes and the whole world goes nuts. Ignoring the obvious paradox (a successful plea for help effectively eliminates the need for help in the first place), the doctors among us know that this is impossible: Prions aren't genetic or airborne. The silent consensus is that someone is terrorizing this impressionable kid for fun. As a sort of final appeal, the boy tells us that time travel is impossible (per the man online), but they can still send information backwards. We've all stopped really listening. There's nothing worse than being up there and getting pity instead of sympathy. It's like staring into the sun. He withers. Somebody claps him on the shoulder as he sits down to examine his hands.

You're probably wondering why we do it. I'm at the meetings three times a week, minimum. It beats portioning out a frozen lasagna to eat alone in front of the TV. What I'm saying is: The concessions are good. Of course, that's not really it—we're not in denial. We know none of this is real, but we can't stop believing. This is the crux of it. So we get together to collect each other's stories and loop them back forever. Or maybe that's just what I do. We don't have a mission statement, and it's not as though we all get together for pub trivia after the fact. The most invested anybody ever gets is a sympathetic glance every now and then. There's a tacit, agreed-upon MO for when you see someone in the real world; you're supposed to ignore them, go figure. I, for example, often see a woman who talks about her husband, a park ranger, who keeps finding doors (just the frames, really, stood upright by god only knows) when he patrols the forest, and she begs him to promise her that he won't go through a single one because she has such a bad feeling

about it, at the supermarket, holding her children's hands and looking generally frazzled as all new parents sometimes do, but I know that going up to her and mentioning the doors would force her to pretend I'm just some crazy woman trying to steal her children or her soul.

It's a routine by now, him and me. Genevieve's ex-husband drops me off outside the hospital, and I feint like I'm going to my car until he's gone. Then I make my way through the hallways until I get to her room.

She hasn't gotten any better, and she's so thin now they've had to tape her rings to her fingers. I slip my wedding band forward and study the dent in my skin. The tan line there looks almost translucent, like a plant grown without light. I still talk to her. I'd admire her stoicism if I thought she'd had any choice in it. She was doing what we all try to do: trying to bargain meaning out of the great cosmic mix-up and coming up empty. Is that a dramatic way to put it? I think of why she's here and decide it isn't.

This last time I was at her house I sneaked off while her ex-husband was in the shower to find the older composition notebooks she'd accumulated. I found what must have been a whole filing cabinet's worth to bring with me and go through now while I sit next to her. This is really the only way I know her. We weren't close before her accident—in fact, during the few words we had exchanged I mostly listened. I pretend, still, that she saw something special in me, as if she thought I could save her. When I'm feeling particularly vindictive I pretend she's done all this as some sort of cruel matchmaking process.

I still haven't mentioned anything to her about her ex-husband and me, though. I don't think he has, either. Probably out of hope that she's still in there. They split right after their kid died, and I can't blame them. There's no coming back from that, is there? That was the whole point of the meetings.

The nurses don't bother with pleasantries anymore. They get right down to it. I stay even when they change Genevieve's bedpan. I know the repulsive ins and outs of being human from watching and, I guess, from living.

You can tell when the meeting is over because somebody gets up to go to the bathroom or to pour herself a cup of coffee. It breaks the spell. The same man who lectured us about Igor Dyatlov and his inexplicably

murdered (?) research team opens up to us about this hotel in Los Angeles where a woman is caught on a malfunctioning elevator's security camera acting strange and talking to someone the camera can't see before she was found dead in the water tower on the roof (only after guests had begun complaining about the water smelling and tasting strange), but even he knows the time has passed. For a second, some woman who has been coming for a month or so halfheartedly starts in on the Mandela Effect again; she and a couple other people meet bi-weekly to discuss a mountain they all remember that just doesn't exist. I don't know where you fall on the whole "Berenstein vs. Berenstain" debate, but when it went mainstream, the Mandela Effect I mean, I thought she was going to have a coronary. She kept telling us she believed first, as if that meant something.

After our closing remarks, there is always a small group milling around out front, talking in hushed tones. You could say, if pressed, that it looks vaguely funereal. It's usually the younger members trying to make sense of the meeting. They treat it academically; to them, the stories (even their own) are something to unpack. Usually, I brush past on my way out and pretend not to hear them start talking about me: the woman whose story they don't know, always at the meeting before they get there. I like to think they usually say something almost cruel but not quite, like "What's so fucked up that she can't tell us?" But tonight I interrupt three men, probably in their twenties, debating furiously among themselves. I target the one who's been coming the longest, just about half a year, and ask for a cigarette. He lights it for me. I ask him if he still has those visions of his past life where he's a WWI soldier named Freckle who's been hospitalized for a gnarly case of gout then begins a classic romance with a nurse from the ward over. He tells me they've just started playing chess as a sort of courtship parable and he's treating it like a lucid dream. He's been studying famous players so he can invent Kasparov before Kasparov's even born—he can't wait to disassociate and see her again. It's affecting his work. His boss will stop him in the hallway and ask how he's doing with parental concern etched into his face. I ask if he's looked for either of these people in the old census records or online, and he says he's afraid to. The other three nod, and I don't say anything after that or really pay attention to the conversation that ensues. Something vague about how one of their girlfriends is experiencing sporadic sleep paralysis that's interfering with

her ability to perform certain sexual acts and whether or not he should "look into other avenues by which to achieve true sexual satisfaction." As if that's why men cheat. When I finish the cigarette, I say a pleasant goodbye and all three of the boys seem satisfied that I'm not a mystery anymore. As I turn to leave, Freckle asks me what happened with that lady that used to come tell us about lights. I pretend not to know what he's talking about and leave them standing there, moving slightly ever so often to keep warm.

Do you know what it's like to see your husband's mistress at his funeral? Let's put it this way: She's the only one I'd wish that on.

Genevieve has been in the hospital for almost three months. I've started feeding her to give the nurses a break. I doubt insurance covers an extended stay like this, but I won't ask her ex-husband about it. We've never discussed Genevieve outside of the hospital, and we won't. She stares straight ahead. If I ask her the right questions, will she answer? Each notebook has the date printed neatly in the center of the first page. The oldest isn't mathematical the way the subsequent ones are; instead, it has pages and pages of single-line hypotheticals: If I had been sick and come home early? If we lived someplace with more sun? If we had talked more?

When their daughter hanged herself, I didn't see Genevieve for two weeks—the longest she'd ever been absent from the meetings. When she returned and no longer left in the middle, I'd figured her daughter had just quit soccer. I didn't even find out that's what had happened until we moved to a wing of the hospital where the nurses' voices carried farther, long after the time to offer condolences and support had passed. I noticed that they never use the word tragedy and chalked it up to what's usually on their schedule.

I'm reading that first notebook aloud to her when I notice her ex-husband standing in the doorway. I don't know how long he's been standing there, but he has this funny expression on his face. Wistful? It's something, at least. He sits down next to me and nods. He tells Genevieve he's sorry and that he loves her. He's at the root of it now. He doesn't avoid the subject and tells her about the two of us. I want to say something that will help, but I can't think of what. Without a word, I pass him the notebook and head home for the first time in weeks.

When I get there I take a shower and wonder about how in love they must have been, once, to get married. I remember my husband—I used to save the parts of letters his tongue touched. He would put my towel in the dryer to warm it up before I finished showering. Where does all that disappear to?

I'm sitting at my kitchen table with two empty bottles of wine and my own notebook. I'm trying to write down the things I remember. The gross smell of Vick's VapoRub before he went to sleep; the time I came home with a bad haircut and wouldn't take off my hood, so he goes out and gets a bad haircut on purpose; when he locks his keys in the car and we spend an hour with fishing wire before either of us bothers to see if he has a spare; the way he used to gnaw pens when he was focused until one exploded in his mouth. The Hierophants. I am only this leftover collection of facts.

Did you know jackdaws can fall in love? He told me that the first night I stayed over. I met him at work, when he wandered into the wrong floor of the wrong building and asked me out to dinner. What if I had called out sick that day? What if he'd double-checked the address? Those go in my notebook, too. I don't like to think about how many universes exist where we'd never met—I don't really understand the science behind it, but the answer is all of them except this one and also, somehow, not all of them? Infinity is beyond comprehension, or at least mine. What are the chances of this happening the way it's happened? All things considered, I'd say one hundred percent.

Low turnout tonight. Maybe half as many people as our most exciting meetings, which makes sense for a weeknight in winter. A lot of members have kids or other obligations. Genevieve used to have to leave midway through to take her daughter to soccer practice. God, that was a lifetime ago. I was newly widowed and trying to take the rules that start off our meetings to heart. Trying to forgive, for instance. Genevieve always made it easy.

I take the podium and think about how she opened that first time. She pulled her brown hair into a messy bun as she rattled off times and locations where she'd seen lights go out above her head. There were so many, I never knew if she was exaggerating. I put my hair up, too. It helps, and, after a moment, I begin:

"After a tarot reading on our honeymoon, my husband and I had a joke: If the Great Danger gets me, I'll come back and haunt you. How

will I know it's you? You'll know. Does that count as a joke? You can figure out the rest, I'm sure. He hasn't shown up yet. The conundrum is obvious. I believe in ghosts and my dead husband hasn't come to see me. Did he go see her? I believe in ghosts and my dead husband might not have loved me as much as I thought he had. How's that for admission?

"It was the most mundane death imaginable. He got hit by a drunk driver. It's almost a cliché by now. I wish it had been some crazy accident on my part, a sleeping pill I give him having an adverse effect or I'm the one driving the other car. Maybe then he comes back. There has got to be criteria for it. Why do all your loved ones show up and terrorize you? He said he would come, and now all I can see are chances that he could make it all up to me. Why are all my clocks still working? When my father's sister died, all his clocks froze for two whole days. Where's his message written in fog on my mirror? Why don't his voicemails change?

"Genevieve's been in the hospital for months now. I've seen them put a tube inside her. I've seen them prick her with needles to test if she'd move. Sometimes the med-school students come by to observe her like a butterfly pinned up on a wall. I've told her things I've never told anyone, and I don't even know if she's in there. Can you imagine if she is? That might be worse.

"That psychic drew the Hierophant card three times and told us whoever succumbs to the Great Danger first will come warn the other. That the Hierophant is always misread as human, but it's the area between here and there, the earthly plane given way to the spectral. Is the Great Danger just living? That'd be rich, but wouldn't he still tell me?

"Go buy a tarot deck online, any of you, and look at that card. His lips press together into a thin, dark line. The meaning is clear: He knows something, but he's keeping his trap shut tight. He's mocking you because he knows the answers. Don't let him. We decide what's real or not and decide the answers. We are the Hierophants."

# BROKE (ALONE) <span style="font-size:small">O'NEILL</span>
## <span style="font-size:small">EMILY</span> AT AMATEUR HOUR

I let a man buy me a drink
tonight & it felt like us / meeting
in reverse / liquid landing

in the wrong hands / how I was
told to call you family / so I trusted
you but guarded my wrists until

we were inside / a snow globe
& you finally fed me something other
than money & hello / told me about

the concert with your brother & outside
all those rabbits & swans / Carrie & Lowell
& understanding death / is a meal

to push around the plate / as it cools
I admired how quiet you got / looking
how swagger / doesn't sit on your shoulders

is there air enough / for what I have yet to say
that you sleep / pulling your beard
like it might come off in your hand

without the disguise / a new life where
I don't have to hide that ghost / photo
of you & the mojito pitcher in my wallet

an unpaid tab / I told that man to assume
there's an arm around me / even when
it's invisible / I am singing

& you once told me / I scratch my nose
in my sleep like a rabbit / I am so happy
to feel soft again / to not be smacked naked

by what someone else wishes I were / a year
to the day I took the interview that carved me
a figurehead for your afternoons

I am braver for your breath / safe enough
to be angry at intruders in real time / air
enough for a new city inside

EMILY O'NEILL

# THE WAY IT DIES

LUKAS RAY HALL

After the bullet

    escapes
    the barrel,

after it snaps

    open throat,
    then lung,

makes blood & tissue

    its new
    family,

my brother & I wade

    through
    the ironwoods

to find it. A stream

    of red smeared
    on the matted-

down silver grass

leads us.
Soon, we find

the deer, pressed

    near-flat
    against the soil.

Heaved in its dying.

    My brother bends
    down. His hands

smooth out the fluffs

    of stray fur.
    Feels the chest

expand, struggle

    to contract,
    the tip of his rifle

making a dig

    at the ground.
    He turns

to me to find that I've

    looked
    away,

that I'm watching the wind

    rattle over
    a branch

of winter buds & pale green

> leaflets,
> & says

*No, no, look.*

> *You have to*
> *learn to love*
>
> *the way*
> *it dies.*

# AIN'T NOTHING CHRISTIAN
## NICK BUT A STRANGER
## IN THIS WORLD

In 1933, Abraham Edwin Christian shot and killed a man. Edwin, by middle name, spent one week in a West Virginian jail cell, married a local girl, had five children, and died fifty-nine years later lying on an Illinois bed in a hill-less town he never, not once, said the name of aloud.

Sometimes names are that muscular; sometimes they grab you, stay in your mouth thick as spoiled marmalade, and never let go. That's why Edwin never said the name of the man he killed aloud, either. The man was only the man, and when he wasn't he was *the fox*, and this fox had its teeth through the feathery neck of a pregnant hen in its first laying year, the best year. This was also the worst year of our Great Depression.

Edwin had stained his coal-miner's finger with that name-stealing trigger at the same time FDR claimed fear was the only thing *to* fear. But that bullet had *boiled* through summer. Boiled hotter than frankness, hotter than vigor. It just moved, moved another late summer into another deep, gasping winter.

Bad winters used to always mean poor living, and there were two things Edwin considered mountain gold when things turned bad: toilet paper and a good pickled egg around the black heat of his wood-burning stove. Well, maybe there were three things. He loved every cracked board of the two-room house he'd built, even as it sunk deeper into the ground beneath a permanently sagged roof, heavy from season after season of lead-foot snows. This was the same roof we would replace for the fifth time when some of us were still wearing all denim and listening to Van Morrison explain what it was like to be home in another land.

It wasn't long after that the stamp of progress, some sixty-two years past hammering in the final nail, slammed down on his home, condemning it, the paperwork claiming it now "unfit for human habitation." Edwin refused to leave until he heard a judge demand it in person, and even then it took both his extended and immediate family's assurances to drag him away. But he got in thick with Appalachian drawl a final promise before leaving that courtroom, and it came in two parts: "Now goddamnit I built it," and, "Goddamnit I'm going to die in it."

A week later he drifted his faded-blue Ford Escort into one of several trees separating a major thoroughfare, sound asleep below a stoplight and the wide, cloudless afternoon sky. Maybe he'd learned to sleep whenever and wherever possible from the war no one seems to remember if he fought. Maybe he was just old and getting older, and maybe it was the coal-miner's blanket that lies over men, gets inside them, and no amount of distance or retirement can shake it.

Breakneck work is like that: It always comes home eventually. Sometimes it gives a boxer dementia; sometimes it gives men like Edwin back a lifetime of exhaustion. He was falling asleep more regularly at irregular, dangerous hours. For everyone's safety he came for keeps to small-town Illinois with his daughter, a grandmother already, and the man she married, whose own father had died half a century ago from an abrupt and lethal fever.

It was at this point seventy-nine-year-old Edwin taught a twelve-year-old boy how to gamble. The card game was called casino, the token chips Werther's Originals, or when things turned serious, sometimes quarters. At that age I was keen on both, so I got good. Learned quick numbers, learned the sly and the liar, but most of all learned that you can build something first and have it taken from you, "And that," Edwin said, "is life." I think buried beneath the slow burr of that voice was a root into what he'd likely say was just "the way it is." It took me a long time to understand that in those words was a warning, a promise that paring down how and what we value most to the novelty of what we do first is a road that chews the feet we walk on. Then again, it's possible he was only bitter about the way his own game was ending.

Edwin said a little about a lot of things, and while there are no jokers in a round of casino, he took their place at the kitchen table, a

master of the sideways compliment or the proverbial saying to ease the pain while he took your cards one after the other. There were three good months of this, one bad, and then no games at all. Time had followed, had filed Edwin down, had ground him until most of what was left were the rotes of his heart, and not of his mind.

Fortunately, good stories live in the chest, and in those later days one was still home in Edwin. He promised if I stood on a clear night beneath Black Rock Mountain in West Virginia, the kind of night that just swallows everything, I would see bands of blue light flowing down from its peak. He said those were the torches of men. Men who'd gone up the mountain after a runaway child in the dark. None of them had returned—none of the men, and no child, either—but he believed they'd never stopped searching for each other. He loved the idea of that, you could see it in the few lucid flashes of his eyes; it was the last song on Edwin's record, so he shared it whenever he surfaced, which was rare. I think a part of Edwin had become the missing child, and another part of him a streak of that light, or it might be he was only a frightened man climbing his mountain in the dark.

When the machines came into his room I saw the way they could attack the spirit—how what's left cries, *Your grief is stealing from me!* After this Edwin seldom had the energy to speak over the noise of his artificial life, but when he did it was to hurl insults at a hospice nurse who ignored them and forced more medication into his body. But this was just trying to put beautiful flowers into a pot common and cracked with long use, one ready to break apart and join another layer of memories covered by dirt.

The day before Abraham Edwin Christian died he kept screaming, "You're trying to kill me! You're trying to kill me!" Maybe he was right. Maybe that's why he never spoke the name of our town. Was this his poison? Was it the soy-field monotony, the flat existence and plains' storms that burned out his body and mind? Or was it because he'd lived a lifetime with a hen in his teeth, watching himself pull a trigger in a room full of his family with the same word on each of their lips: *peacefully*.

# THE DOG ARZAH
## AHOLAAH IS A GHOST

The dog is just a ghost this morning, inextricable from the breeze off the water. I am looking at the small slow wisps of vapors that are curling up, stray tufts of white hair on the shining bald pate of the pond and I notice that the dog is nowhere. I was certain that he brushed my legs as I opened the door to the deck but when I returned with my coffee there were only the empty weatherworn planks.

At least twice in the small space of this reluctant morning he has disappeared. He passed me headed down the hall as I filled his water bowl but when I later looked for him, convinced that he had gone to drink from the toilet, the hall and the bathroom were empty. As I write, there is a boisterous routing sound beneath the window but when I stealthily draw back the curtain there are only two small black birds hurling themselves into the gatherings of dry leaves and needles.

The dog was here; I know this. While I heated the water for coffee, he leaned into my legs and I stroked his head. There was, I felt, an air of sadness to his demeanor that caused me to wonder if I had remembered to feed him the night before. As so often happens these days, I could not separate the impression of all the cumulative feedings; how I picked up the bowl and added the kibble, how I shredded a bit of cheese or tore a few strips of chicken from the carcass to top his meal, from the actual events of the previous evening. It seems as though my life goes on living itself in repetitions where perhaps the dog is not the only ghost.

The dog is given to some unpredictable flares of aggression toward other dogs, so we drive past the dog park, our former haunt. Actually, I think every one of these occurrences of aggression defensible. The black she-mutt snapped in his face. It was a quick and sly assault that went without witness from the owner. And the large German

Shepherd puppy just required a curb to his enthusiasm, a reminder of his status. The owners over-identify, are excessively involved. It's primal; it's just dog stuff. Nevertheless, we have found another place to walk in the mornings. The business park development with its open fields of potential opportunity is almost uninhabited. There are places to run, ducks to chase, and a pond with cattails. Significantly secluded on the farthest back loop, tucked up against the adjoining woods and bordered by blackberry fragrant brambles, is Mental Health Services.

Lately the dog and I have been intersecting with some of the clients, adolescent males in particular. I come across them sitting on the dirt and gravel edge where the asphalt ends and the ground becomes ferns and grasses. They are fiddling with the wheels on their skateboards, looking dejected and recalcitrant. I make a point of intrusion, of saying *Hello*. I think it is probably important to acknowledge them even if their response is muted and sullen. I can tell a lot about them just by the tone of that response, how grudgingly it's given up, whether they will make eye contact. Sometimes it makes me a little nervous to interact with them, so maybe my greeting is really an offensive action meant to disarm. Most of the time they don't seem too dangerous, just depressed, just kind of messed up.

Other young men, with their rapid robotic stride, pace the perimeter of the business park. When they pass me, they hunch their shoulders and drop their heads, the whole of their self visibly retracts the way a snail's eyestalks shrivel to the touch of a fingertip. I do not greet these; there is too much contained there under pressure. These or the others, they all walk here from various parts of our small town. I see them in my routine comings and goings out by North Beach or headed downtown on Water Street. It is probably a part of their therapists' prescribed treatment. Walking it out. I know that it works for me. Each morning I wake to rifle through the new day's particular bag of knives. I have to find ways to counter those nettling pricks and nicks. It is not just the dog that needs a walk.

One of the young men lollops with his Converse-clad feet slightly turned out, swaggering in his black jeans and T-shirt, his short-cropped dark hair, his brown eyes and designer-frame glasses. I think about how his mother must love him, must love his blemish-enraged skin, his condescending gaze framed by the glasses she so obviously picked out for him. I had just called the dog back from his investigation of something likely malodorous when we happened to pass. The young

man sneers, *Was the dog being too slow?* And then he spits.

*Who is it who is so impatient with you?* I counter.

The dog is chasing the ducks, churning up some duck adrenaline fueled alarm, but it is not as though he can actually catch them. I think it is probably good for the ducks not to become too complacent. On my way this morning I passed converse-shod-guy-who-spits about a half a mile from the park. He was dancing his way down the road and just as I passed, he did a little hip dip and spun himself around. Evidently life has not yet left him completely dispirited.

Now here he is, coming across the field, and unfortunately it appears we are going to intersect. Yesterday he yelled at the dog to stay back although the dog was nowhere near him and was occupied nosing through the rough stubble of some yellowed grass. I slow my pace while hoping to avoid the encounter, but he is matching his pace to mine. When I pause and chuck a stick for the dog, spit guy stops to adjust his shoelaces. When we are close enough to speak he says, *That was your car.* One of the cars that passed him this morning was mine, so I agree. *Yeah, that was my car.* He is swaggering again, bobbling along beside me as though he has loosened all his joints, as though he is a marionette, each movement slightly suspended in air, directed by another hand. *So I am going this way and you are going this way.* The statement dangles as though it too has strings. I realize that he is asking for a ride and taken off guard by this, I find myself agreeing to this as well.

Right away I start thinking about how I could possibly be some kind of older, wiser mentor, but then I think I could be way cooler than that and just be someone who gives him a ride, but then I begin to regret my assent because really I should have asked, *Do you think that it's OK with your parents? Do you think it's OK with your therapist?* Because the walking is probably a part of his therapy and I'll be screwing that up, and who knows what precise proportion of walking to talking is required to maintain whatever it is that is being maintained? And just what is being maintained? He could be one of those highly manipulative kids with maleficent intent. He could be one of those really desperate kids who doesn't even know his own intent. I realize I am more than a little afraid of meeting up with any desperate, unknown, maleficent intents. It is obviously time for the dog and me to move along. We are uncomfortable with overfamiliarity. We are uncomfortable with encroachments. Somewhere there must

be another little-used park, another empty field to tread without the disturbance of interactions. Why, I wonder, is it always so difficult just to find a quiet place of our own to let a big dog off the leash?

# I WAS FOURTEEN <span style="font-size:smaller">CEDAR</span>
## <span style="font-size:smaller">ROBIN</span> WHEN I FOUND THE SHOE

on the beach, Adidas size 11,
        and when I opened the sock
                there was a foot inside.

                Back home, I drifted
        from room to room switching
on lights, closing my eyes, then opening

them again once I saw waterlogged
        men missing only their left feet.
                I waded through the house

                for days without bathing,
        encased in a blue comforter
and unable to sleep.

My mother found me in her closet
        counting out the shoes. *Honey*,
                she said, kneeling with one

                foot planted, the other
        foot tucked underneath her.
*All of them are there.*

My body turned into a crab cage
        where all my thoughts crawled
                inside and could not leave again.

When I was younger still,
I pretended to be a mermaid.
I dove beneath the surface,

never thinking of my body,
how it can only take in
so much salt and water,

never realizing that, given time,
my weak ankle joints might rot away
and my feet might drift to the surface.

How they might float away
from me, only to be found
by a little girl on a beach far away.

ROBIN CEDAR

## DEAN
## REARING

DEBRA KANG

When a donkey sits down
as if to say, I shall not be moved,
we call it stubborn.

And yet, on Palm Sunday
and once before, Jesus rode
on the back of a donkey.

In moving forward
headfirst, animals go
and the body follows.

Has one gone wild standing up
as a horse does, the one
we say is rearing?

When marsh water sucks back
the muskrat, an eagle
circles one last time,

lights on the back
of its catch then holds fast,
breaststroking shoreward.

When a hooked fish flexing
its body left and right points
its head skyward and breaks

## REARING

the surface, we admire the leap
but keep our eyes trained forward,
remembering only the nails

protruding, hammered down.

DEBRA KANG DEAN

# OUT OF BO(U)NDS

DEAN
DEBRA KANG

*... to humanise even the enemy*
—Mahmoud Darwish

When you put up a wall, you've effectively drawn
two sides. If you add four more, you can create
a space that will shape what does and doesn't belong
inside—moths, for example, or flies, gnats.

Adding to two sides four more will complicate
any argument. No doubt, you'll have made a wilderness
that discloses, like moths, flies, or gnats,
a shape to repulse the mind. Call it a tangled mess

because when argument sprawls into a wilderness,
someone will often call for Occam's razor to simplify
into an easily apprehended shape that tangled mess—
think hair tamed by a blunt cut. No more beehives.

When calling on Occam's razor to simplify,
why not also invoke that other blade, the guillotine.
No hair splitting—or, rather, one clean cut. The beehive's
contentious buzzing will stop. Like that, finé.

Sometimes people invoke knowledge, like a guillotine.
(A real discussion stopper.) How can one not feel snakebit
by the venom of gossip that ensues. Like that, finé,
a self-appointed umpire has called the third strike: Out.

Knowledge can sting. How does one not feel snakebit?
It's a story going all the way back to Eden with God
a designated umpire-in-chief calling the third strike: Out.
No Great Writ for this story of possessed, clay-hewn bodies.

In one version of the story of paradise, preachers cast God
as a father who, prizing above all else obedience,
claims absolute possession of his children's bodies,
thus setting the bar for their very un-Edenic existence.

In the name of a fatherland prizing obedience
a guard at the Juarez/El Paso border scrutinizes passports,
stripping the holder, honest or not, of her own existence.
In a game of us and them, it's sadly a full-court press.

Long ago, a customs officer eyed my driver's license,
said, "You don't look American." I know an Asian Asian
playing this game would mark me in an instant
by my slouch. What did I do? I smiled, said nothing.

I'm obviously not all-American. I'm not Hawaiian
either though the fact is I grew up near Papakolea,
a slouch, an outsider who rarely smiled, said nothing
in a world that was bewilderingly multilayered.

I was a neither, growing up near Papakolea.
See how early the via negativa circumscribed my life,
raised as I was in a world so deeply multilayered,
nothing anyone tells me about it can quite describe it.

A playwright's via negativa begins with a polished script.
Later, the fourth wall, a curtain, opens, is a window.
Everything said or done on stage becomes inscription
of the interior's hall of mirrors and its shadows.

Imagination can turn a fourth wall into a window,
make of the mind a theater where everything belongs.
Shining its light in dimly lit places, it dispels shadows.
It is the well inside the self from which we must draw.

75

# MONOLOGUE FOR FLO POLILLO, EMMA JOHNSON-RIVARD THIRD VICTIM OF THE BUTCHER OF KINGSBURY RUN (1936)

Like with the others, it was a woman who found the body. It was usually a woman or a group of young boys, or girls dressed in boys' clothing, who found them, though no one gave it much thought or bothered to learn their names. Who they were hardly mattered compared to what they found. Knowing their names would have involved knowing their lives in some small but unavoidable way, and that was not done. This was 1936, Cleveland, and pain was contagious. To know a stranger's life, even the smallest piece, was to risk inhaling the dust of their daily bread and all the hungry pains it wrought. Only the dead were immune, and, as such, their stories were safe for human consumption. So it goes. The dead are gone and so their stories belong to everyone, or no one, whichever; either way, they mean whatever you want them to mean. It's very easy to mold the dead. But in the end it was a woman who found it outside the Hart Manufacturing Building on Central Avenue, by the East 20th Street Junction. Does it matter what she was doing there? No one wrote that part down. It's probably not important. What she found does matter, though—in most ways, more than anything else. In that moment, it carried more weight to history than the sum of her life, and this woman—not a witness but a player in the tale, somebody—saw a dog eating a something out of a basket by the side of the road. She thought it was a leg of ham at first and chased the dog off for a better look. There was a second basket sitting there right next to the first, with pieces of meat wrapped in newspaper, and she looked inside this one too. Why? It's not said. Maybe she was

curious. More likely she knew the value of meat and not to waste an opportunity. Maybe her name was Sarah and two baskets of ham, even the kind half eaten by dogs, could have brought some money from her neighbors, the ones who hoarded sugar in the lean times. In Cleveland those lean times stretched on for years, and in America that made Sarah's neighbors both clever and quick with their money. Perhaps she had a sibling, too. A brother, let's say, handsome as they go and two years younger, and that brother—let's call him Eli, that's a good name for Sarah's brother—*well*. He still laughed at things, the kind of laughter you didn't have to work at, and hadn't yet gone bitter over his lot in life. Let us not forget this was Cleveland and this was the Depression; a person suffered if they weren't rich, and rich girls don't go sniffing around through baskets of old ham on Central Avenue. But this girl did, this sister of Eli; she bent down and got a good look in. Maybe she was thinking about neighbors with their secret tins of sugar and how they'd trade for things out the back window, whatever you had but didn't quite need, and maybe then she thought about her laughing brother, with his birthday coming up and what happens to folks when they stop smiling, when there's nothing to expect in the morning but more of the same. Maybe she thought about cleaning that ham up and trading it for some sugar and eggs, some cocoa, too, if the neighbors were feeling generous, and that wouldn't feed the house but it would make a nice cake, wouldn't it? It's not much of a birthday without a cake, and it doesn't take much to make one, not really. And that's the thing history forgets, that people were still alive back then. There were bad times, but they passed, and people went on as people do. So maybe this girl was named Sarah, for her grandmother, and maybe when Sarah looked in the basket she thought about her brother turning twelve and how he'd smile when he made that birthday wish over her cake. It's important to make wishes when you're young. They might still come true. So she looks in the basket. Just the first one, where the dog tore the newspapers to get at it. Maybe she's thinking about how she can cut the teeth marks out, save the rest. Sarah's a survivor. She's still alive and so she's smart, so maybe she's smiling when she looks inside, thinking about good times. Brothers and birthdays and dancing candle flame.

Maybe she screamed then. Probably she screamed. If you know anything you can probably guess it wasn't ham. Maybe she cried.

EMMA JOHNSON-RIVARD

Maybe it took her a while to notice. She's clever, fine, she's beautiful and clever in that thin way survivors are, but she's kind, too, Sarah is, and people like that don't walk down the street thinking human beings can be split down the middle and fitted into baskets on Central Street. They don't think about women named Florence being murdered and broken, their dignity gone just like their heads. Like the head, the dignity probably proved hard to find afterward. Maybe Sarah didn't know anyone named Florence or a man with tattoos on his knuckles or any of the others those women and wandering boys found out in the swamp, but she could have known the waitress who worked down the road, the old woman with too many lovers and not enough time, or maybe she really did know the prostitute called Flo Polillo that the papers wrote about. People did know her, Flo or Florence, whatever you like; she had a life and found it taken, but sometimes we care more about the sex she sold, the bad company we suppose she kept. What an awful, ugly woman. A great deal was written about her looks. They called her ugly but she wasn't. I found a picture someone took when she was alive. She had curls, you know? The kind you take care of. But I know Sarah didn't see those curls, not that morning anyway, because someone else found her head in a vacant lot afterward, the rest of her spread around. He did that, the murderer; he did it to a lot of other people and we still don't know all their names. Maybe Sarah didn't know Flo, but I like to think she learned it afterward, that she remembered this woman had a name and it meant more than meat in a basket, a life wrapped in paper and eaten by dogs. Flo Polillo died a person, despite what was done, what was written about it. She was a person with a name, a beautiful name. Florence Genevieve Polillo. It's English, you know, short for St. Florentina. The saint's bones are kept in Mureia, Spain. They're considered holy relics. I don't know what Flo's bones were called. Tragic, maybe.

Florence also comes from *florentius*, or "blossoming," and the verb *floreo*, which means "to flower." So, in a way, Flo Polillo came from holy women and wreathes of flowers. Maybe Sarah put flowers on her grave. Maybe she made it beautiful.

She was the third, Flo Polillo, and there were more after her. No one was made to account for it and no one remembers her now, except perhaps Sarah and the children she passed her kindness down to. I like to think they remembered the woman with the curls, named

for flowers and holy women. I like to think they named her beautiful, *belle morte*, a lovely ghost, that they gave her words and a new story. I hope someone remembers.

# BY FRITH
## SUSAN THE BLACK GUM TREE

She's got rough hands, Phoebe's mama does—crack between thumb and forefinger, scar where the snake bit her, scar where the whip marked her—but this morning they're playing with a silky, yellow ribbon cast off from the mistress's sewing kit. Ribbon thin as sweetgrass, tied end to end.

Her mother's hands weave and dance, one finger borrowing from another. Crisscross. Palms squeeze shut, and loops drop from thumbs to wrists. Palms open and thumbs pull another string onto their backs. When her mother's sure that Phoebe's watching, she draws the ribbon nice and tight to show off her trick.

"What's it called?"

"Four stars," her mama tells her, and with a sigh like the wind shaking the palmettos outside their cabin, she pulls the shape apart.

Phoebe hates to see it turn back into nothing. "Show me another."

Her mother smiles sleepily. "Here's one I learned when I was a girl. Might even need your toes for this."

Giggling, Phoebe rises from the flour-sack pillow that smells like her mama, like five kinds of medicine, and slides her feet out from under the scratchy blanket. No sooner has she done this when someone bangs on the door.

Phoebe dives back under the blanket, wondering if it's angry knock or want-something knock. Hardly ever happy knock. When her papa gets a pass to visit from the next plantation, he chirps like a purple martin outside their cabin because he knows the knocks scare her—even worse, the door creaking open in the dark for Mr. Turner, the master's brother, who comes in reeking of snuff and rosewater. Phoebe's mother does the healing around the rice plantation, even

on the white folks sometimes, but Mr. Turner needs a special kind of doctoring. He pulls her mother into a corner, grunting softly while he takes his medicine.

This time, it's only the overseer's ten-year-old son, practicing his ordering-around voice as he tells them that the best field hand's sick. "You need to fix him right."

When he's gone Phoebe's mother stands on a crate and pulls down a small, green bundle from the ceiling. Not much left.

They hurry-walk to the woods, which are plenty awake by now. A speckled, brown spider works on its own string trick for Phoebe, while a frog springs across her path to hide in a clump of ferns. The deeper they go, the fiercer the flies. Phoebe smacks her neck, wiping a smear of blood on the bark of a black gum tree. Then something else catches her attention, something with big, veiny leaves popping out of the ground to say hello.

She points. "Is it here?"

"No." Her mama grabs her hand. "This here's skunk cabbage," she warns. "Smell that stalk. It's poison, much of it anyway." Phoebe shrinks back.

"Plants are a lot like people," her mother explains. "Some'll help you. Some'll hurt. And some—." She shakes her head. "It just depends."

Phoebe walks on, parting briars, quick-stepping over the spongy ground, keeping her eyes on the swamp, which wears a bright-green blanket to hide the creatures that might suck her in. A woodpecker taps on a cypress trunk, sending down chunks of bark onto the leaves of—she stops again. "Down here?"

Her mama gives her a squeeze. "Good girl! You must've been listening to me." They reach down and pull.

When they get back to the cabin, Mr. Turner is waiting. "I need some salve for my hands," he tells her mama. "I need it right now," he says, and even though Phoebe hasn't eaten, he sends her to the fields to chase away the rice birds. As the door shuts she thinks of her mother in the corner. She thinks of the skunk cabbage, too.

She won't forget the spot where it grows—by the black gum tree. Her secret in the woods.

81

# THE PIETRZYK
# FAVORITE
LESLIE

**1975**

Lexie wants a horse. A horse is the only solution and could be a friend, worrying with her how she sits alone at lunch, that they whisper "Pudgerina" to her back. Or, if she has a horse, possibly they'd talk nice to her. A horse is dramatic, but it's the only way out.

Her father is the one to make the decision. Doesn't matter a whit if her mother thinks getting a horse is the most magnificent idea in the world or if the principal sends home a typed note on school stationery in a sealed envelope recommending the horse. Doesn't even matter if God himself commands that a horse appear. Only her father will decide.

She puts off asking. He's been trapped in a crummy mood lately, his face blotchy and puffed pink when he gets home from his office at the bank, as if he spent the day yelling nonstop. She's sitting quietly in the corner, no lights on, TV notched low; volume is irrelevant while soap operas bleed into sitcom reruns that blur into hair-sprayed heads droning about faraway problems. She barely notices the screen, eyeing instead the flickering shadows of light tiptoeing up the walls as she waits for her stomach to unclench after her day at school, each day taking a little longer. One day it won't unclench at all, she imagines. Then what?

Last week her mother hissed that she was "daddy's little favorite," which is dizzying information. How can this be? He never joins her in front of the TV. Instead, he leans in the archway dividing the TV room from the kitchen, gazing into her hazy gloom, not speaking, simply staring like a statue someone placed and forgot. She doesn't twist to glance over her shoulder at him; she doesn't acknowledge him at all. Instead, she pretends to herself she doesn't know he's there,

though she feels his presence the way she feels the heaviness of her head balanced at the top of her spine. Is he looking at her? The shadows? The TV? Maybe something else entirely, a thing in the room she's unable to see. He doesn't allow them to believe in ghosts, so not that exactly. But maybe that feeling. There's the moment where she can't stand it one second more, so she says, "Hey, Daddy," and as easy as can be, he "hey"s right back, then turns to the kitchen to grab the martini pitcher from the freezer. It's like he can't remember who she is until she speaks. Like he's trying to figure out who she belongs to, like he doesn't know she's his, or that, actually, all of this, everything he looks at, is his.

Every day until today feels like the day before she'll ask about the horse, or possibly the day before the day before. In that stretch of time where she's pretending he's not there when he actually is, she thinks about the words she might say and how remarkable it could all be if he just agreed. Today is different, suddenly, because today as she's waiting—can I get a horse swirling the inside of her skull—he says, "Come with me," and her insides do that familiar lurch, like dropping down into a new, uncomfortable position, and she immediately jumps up and follows him into the kitchen. "Sit down," he says, so she does, at the breakfast counter, sitting straight like a lady on the high stool, like how her mama always nags her to.

"Want a martini?" he asks, opening the freezer door. There's the frosty white pitcher that her mother mixed ten minutes ago, after the phone call saying he's on the way. The long, slim spoon between her mother's fingers had tinkled briskly.

She's paralyzed by his question, as she felt that first time she saw the ocean, two years ago, with waves clawing the surf. The roar echoed thunder in her ears; a hurricane was rolling up the coast, and instead of canceling vacation ("...like any normal person," her mother hissed), her father drove her to the Outer Banks anyway so she could see the ocean for the first time, as promised—so she could see this. "The true nature of an ocean," her father explained. The hurricane swung off-shore, so no grave danger, but still. She was oddly ashamed that her father had done this to her, and she never told anyone. The little boys stayed home with Mama. Only she got dragged out to witness that surging, slithering water. "Don't you love it?" her father said, grasping her hand tightly as if she might break free and plunge her body deep into that churn, which of course she knew not to. "Don't you feel alive seeing this?" When she couldn't answer, he said, "I sure as hell do," and

that embarrassed her, too. Back home, her mother asked what they did at the beach, and she said, "Looked at the water," and her mother said, "That's all?" and she nodded, because that was true but also a lie.

Now this. Does she want a martini? Does she?

"OK." She speaks cautiously, in case it's a trap. Her mother is upstairs. She likes to sit in the playroom with the boys and watch them drive tiny toy cars around and around and around a plastic orange track.

He strides to the hutch and pulls out a second glass that matches the glass in the freezer. She's forbidden to touch these glasses when she washes dishes.

"I like olives in mine," he says.

"I know." Plenty of times she has seen her mother pluck those jars off the grocery store shelf. "Me, too," she says.

"Good," he says.

He retrieves the long silver spoon from the sink and tinkles it in the pitcher. That sound again. Like being an adult. "Always, always stir a martini," he says. "Please don't ever shake it."

"OK." Her voice sounds tinny in her own ears. She rests her hands flat on the grainy surface of the breakfast bar. It's not sticky, though breakfast was frozen waffles and Aunt Jemima syrup. Her mother wipes everything clean the second forks are set down. Her father was already at the office then, only a cup half-full of dark coffee to show he had been here, abandoned in the upper right of his place mat, which is the lemon. Lexie's is the apple. Her mother gets the orange, and the boys fight over the grapes and the banana. No one wants the lemon, so that's how her father gets it. Place mats, too, are wiped immediately after each meal. Right now, they're on the dining room table, which Lexie carefully sets, one of her chores before being allowed to turn on the TV. Something half-made's already in the fridge, a casserole or meatloaf. They aren't like regular families, eating right when the father comes home. They eat late, at eight o'clock or nine, and sometimes the little boys are squirmy and sometimes they fall asleep under the table and her father carries them up to bed, both at the same time.

He says, "Is this your first martini?"

"Well, yeah," she says. "I think so."

"You think so?"

"Unless maybe I drank one when I was a baby," she says.

He laughs. His laugh is solid, like something to grab hold of. He laughed that time at the ocean, laughed a whole lot. "Well, you might

not like it right at first," he says. "But you're getting to be such a big girl now that I bet you'll surprise me. What are you now, young lady, twenty-six-and-a-half years old?"

Her turn to laugh. It's a bit they do, where he pretends not to know how old she is. "I'm ten," she says.

All the while, he's been tinkling the martini, and now he stops. "Did you see how delicate I stirred?" he says. "Be like that, in whatever you do, delicate and conscious. Don't whipsaw your hand around," and he mimes an imitation of her mother stirring: too fast, eyes rolling crazily, churning up the invisible martinis.

He pops open the olive jar, and their briny scent invades the room. "Some people say two, but I say let's stick with the classic," he says, "because too many people go around trying to change things," and he maneuvers the spoon to the bottom of the jar to dredge out two olives, letting one plunk into each glass.

"This is the life," he says, pouring clear, almost shiny liquid into the cone-shaped glasses until it quivers to a stop halfway up. "Cheers," he says, lifting the glass, tilting it toward her.

Instead of picking up the martini, she speaks: "Daddy, can I get a horse?" She's abrupt, speaking too fast. Not at all the way she planned. But the words are out and she can't put them back in, something her mother is always saying, warning her to think before she talks, think before she bothers anyone with what she might need.

"Honey, I said, 'Cheers,'" and her father motions his glass upwards. "Don't leave me hanging." A prickly undercurrent that she recognizes.

She clutches the glass by its long, thin stem. The top-heaviness of it is wobbly in her hand, and she concentrates on not spilling. The two glasses tink, exactly the way she's watched adults tink wineglasses at the table and on TV. Her glass is the one from the freezer, and it's icy cold between her fingers. The olive rolls and bobs at the bottom, like a loose eyeball, she thinks. The red pimento gazes straight at her, warning her. What will happen if she drinks this martini? What could happen, with her father right here, with her the favorite and the horse question finally out in the open, and her father in this very good mood? What could possibly go wrong? She smiles at him, and he opens up his whole entire smile to her, just like that, and it's like the world starts spinning for real, and she absolutely can't wait to see what comes next. Something good, something as magnificent as a horse but better. She is suddenly certain.

# (MARY) LEJEUNE

DANÈLLE **CELESTE**

My body is a ghost ship, seaworthy at half sail.
The captain's quarters undisturbed, the bedsheets
folded at the corners, silk pillows at the head.
Cargo still stacked up, neatly down below,
decks washed clean with salt and spit, not a soul on deck.

It is terrible luck to carry a woman on a ship like this.
I carry this woman here, hidden, so there were two aboard.
The sail runs up, with a white flag, made of lace and satin,
tied at the neck with pearls and something blue.

A man downstairs, calls for his supper.
Laundry whips on the line. Adrift in the wide open sea.
The teakettle rattles at boil. Screen doors slam.
My body is a ghost ship. Mutiny. Mutiny. Mutiny.

KALIDEN
ROSALIND **ROT**

*—after* The Return of Judith to Bethulia,
*c. 1472, by Sandro Botticelli*

The ugliness of the world is a severed head
peeking through the wire of a woven basket,
the yellow skin, the dark blood-clotted beard,
the trophy head at the top of a pike.

My feet are rough.
I watch the crows pull out the hair
of the head I held in my hands
and make a nest in the city trees.

While the men slept in the village,
I wore my golden beads, perfumed my hands,
and took my slave, who wove
a silver fillet in my hair, past the walls.

The soldiers hadn't bathed in weeks,
the half-turned meat sweated in the cooks' tent.
They cut off our water for days, and I bathed in the rain.
I brought food and water to the enemy general's tent.
I left with his scimitar in my hand.

# GHOST EXHIBIT 4.1

MELISSA ATKINSON MERCER

they said you were black but not too black//they said your brother was black//very black//as when he split the kitchen table with an axe// as when he emptied the walls with his hands//& what came out// what always comes out//they said my brother was not black enough// Oreo//half-breed//ruined milk//as when he peeled back the walls of his arms like the peaches we spent all summer boiling into jam// they said yes my sister could be black//but she had to choose//choose now//they said do any of you even know//your real parents//did your mother leave you in a basket in the market//did your father turn to smoke behind bars//like my brother//shooting at soda cans with his five white friends & I'll leave you to guess//which one they took

# CONFEDERATE FLAG SHOT GLASS

JOSHUA MICHAEL STEWART

I've used it to fill a syringe with a syrupy laxative
    that I'd squirt down my cat's throat.
A roadside trinket my stepdad gave to me.
A what-the-fuck-you-have-that-for conversation piece.
        A bit of home to wrap my hand around.
    As a friend says about the mill town
he grew up in, *It's a shithole, but it's my shithole.*

   Is it evidence?
         My roots are hillbilly, I'm already suspect.
Sure, I've said it.
        I was raised to say it as commonly as, *Pass the salt.*

I went with my mother to lay dollar-store flowers
    on my brother's grave.
Getting out of the car she said, *Lock up.* I said, *Why?*
       *Are the dead going to crawl*
*out of the ground and steal your Toyota?*
       And she said, *Naw, blacks live nearby.*

Moments later, we're looking down at my brother's name cut
into flat stone. My arms wrapped around her as she wept.
    *You were a good mom. You did good, you did good.*

     Medieval monks rested skulls
on their writing desks to confront immortality.
Is this why I've held on to the shot glass—a vigilance
    against my upbringing?

*Walk like a white man.*
*Do it right like a white man.*
*Speak like a white man.*

Everyone used to say, *You look just like your mother.*

Truth and the fear of truth.

What's been bred within my breed?
The world was born for men like me to be born.
Nothing matters
until we take part in it, unless we own it.

What I've learned and fail to learn?
It's when we should shut our mouths we speak.

JOSHUA MICHAEL STEWART

# LOOKING FOR ETHEL

KARLA KEFFER

My mother is combing my hair one night as we watch a Channel 13 documentary called *The Unquiet Death of Julius and Ethel Rosenberg*. Tonight is the thirtieth anniversary of their execution. My mother is amazed that I didn't know this, although I am only seven years old. She hits another snarl and I wince. She taps the side of my head with the comb, none too gently. She snaps at me to hold still. I protest that it hurts. She tells me if I complain again, she's going to shave it off.

We live in the East Village, in a third-floor walk-up on Avenue A and East 9th Street, a railroad flat with a bathtub in the kitchen and holes in the ceiling. Because she is a cellist by training, my mother fancies herself bohemian, although we are actually poor; thanks to arthritis in her hands, my mother hasn't worked in months. Our only financial relief comes in the form of checks from my rich grandparents in Virginia. This is better than most of the neighbors, who are forced to live on welfare, but it isn't good, especially since my mother spends a large chunk of our money on things like Joan Baez records and scallops from Citarella. It's enough, however, for my mother to maintain her superiority, although since she likes to believe she's a liberal, she tempers her neighborly scorn with a tight-lipped smile.

Although it's only the middle of June, summer's fetid stew has set in, and my mother has moved the TV into her bedroom, which is the only air-conditioned room in the apartment. I sleep on the floor in there most nights. Occasionally, my mother will be so magnanimous as to allow me in bed with her, but I am a restless child, and I never know when I'm going to lose control of my extremities and accidentally kick my mother in the ribs before she banishes me to the floor again. She says I snore, too, and she's threatened to tape-record me to prove it.

My mother forces me to watch the documentary with her. She says it's important for me to learn how the world works. It's not lost on me that Ethel Rosenberg looks like my mother, pale and heavy and unsmiling. I ask what she did, and my mother says she and her husband Julius were accused of spying for the Soviet Union. I know about the Soviet Union; it's a terrible place where people have to stand in line for days to buy toilet paper, and I have a rudimentary knowledge of espionage from *Harriet the Spy*. I ask why anyone would spy for them, and my mother says they didn't, that was just what that bastard David Greenglass told the government. I ask my mother what a bastard is, and she says it's a term used to describe awful people like David Greenglass and under no circumstances am I to repeat the word, especially around my grandparents. I ask her what makes David Greenglass so awful, and she says he murdered his sister. I ask if he used a gun, and she says no and admonishes me to pay attention. I try, but it's not long before the narrator's somnambulant voice lulls me to sleep.

My mother sleeps until noon on a good day, so in the morning I pad out to the hot kitchen and pour myself a glass of orange juice and a bowl of Pathmark no-frills Cheerios. I do the dishes from the night before, praying to an ambiguous godhead that this might stave off my mother's wrath at whatever crimes she's decided I've committed that day. Since I am not allowed to leave the apartment unless my mother is awake, I take *Harriet the Spy* out on the fire escape and watch the people in the streets, the bodega owners and junkies who, even now, are giving way to hipsters and art galleries, although I don't think much about that then.

The next time I see Ethel Rosenberg, it's about a week later, in the window of P.S. 122, when we're on our way to B&H Dairy to buy lox and bagels. There is a large photo of her in the prison van with Julius, looking even grimmer than I remember her. Scrawled across the bottom, in red spray paint, are the words WE REMEMBER. My mother is very excited. She reminds me these are the people from the documentary we saw last week. She runs her fingers along the glass as if this were the *Mona Lisa*. An alarmingly skinny young man with a safety pin in his right ear and a purple splotch on his cheek opens the door and asks if we would like to come in. I whine about being hungry. My mother clamps my shoulder hard and says we live

in the neighborhood and we'll be back. When we're out of earshot, she tells me to stay away from people with purple splotches on them, that they're very sick and they could be contagious. She says there are a lot of people like that in this neighborhood and I'll have to be careful.

The line at B&H is long, full of punks and old Jewish women alike. I amuse myself by finger-spelling the alphabet and counting silently to twenty in Spanish, like I've learned from *Sesame Street*. The cashier is a gentle old man in aviator glasses. He offers me a free egg cream but my mother tells him no, thank you.

We stop at a newsstand, and my mother buys a copy of *The New York Times*. I hate the *Times* because it has no comics and because my mother spends hours analyzing the news and I'm not allowed to talk to her. As we're leaving, we run into her friend Mimi, who lives on East 11th Street. I like Mimi for her root-beer-colored spiral curls and because she talks to me like I'm a person, not a seven-year-old. Mimi gives me a hug and tells my mother about an article in the paper about the East Village gallery scene. They talk about something called gentrification, and they agree that since the *Times* is writing about the East Village, the neighborhood is done. I ask what gentrification is, and my mother says it's the process of making neighborhoods too nice for people like us to live in them. I say this neighborhood isn't nice, and they both laugh and Mimi says ruefully, "Just you watch, kiddo."

We eat pierogies and cold cucumber soup from Veselka for dinner, and my mother tells me about another article in the Times about a movement to extend the presidential term to six years instead of four. My mother thinks this is a terrible thing. She says we're practically living under a dictatorship with the likes of Ronald Reagan anyway, and to extend the presidential term to six years would make that manifold. Occasionally, my mother talks to me like I'm a person, not a seven-year-old, but she expects me to know exactly what she's talking about, and when I don't she reverts to talking to me like I'm a seven-year-old and not a very smart one at that. She says it's assholes like Ronald Reagan that saw to it the Rosenbergs were executed, that the prosecutor, Roy Cohn, is a friend of Reagan's and he's the one who convinced Ethel's brother to tell those awful lies about her that sent her to the electric chair. I ask my mother why he did that, and she says that the Rosenbergs were easy targets because people wanted a fair and just America and they had to blame someone. She says that what happened to the Rosenbergs could still happen today, that money

talks and bullshit walks. I ask what that means, and she says it means that people like us have to live in the East Village while assholes like Ronald Reagan get to live in the White House.

I have no idea what my mother is talking about, but I am thrilled to be a part of her "us," even if that means living in the East Village, because there is no greater sin than being an idiot, and, besides, Ronald Reagan and his preternaturally big head terrify me. When she wants to, my mother is capable of giving me the world in twelve-dimensional Technicolor; this is one of those times, and I know to lean up against it, to lap it up, drop by drop, before the curtain descends again. And it will descend; my grandparents' check will be late or another gig will fall through or the wind will blow wrong, and I'll be expected to absorb the shift in mood with a smile on my face.

In my bath that night, I try to digest everything my mother has told me, but the only thing I can remember is "Money talks and bullshit walks." I say it softly. It's the first time I've ever cursed. It feels so good to say "bullshit" that I repeat it over and over until I hear my mother walking towards the kitchen and I dunk my head under water.

The night before the 4th of July, someone throws a brick through the window of P.S. 122. We find this out the next day when we're walking to Mimi's for a rooftop picnic. My mother stops to talk to another skinny young man with a safety pin in his ear, one without a purple splotch on his cheek. He tells my mother that someone left a message on their answering machine about that Communist cunt, Ethel Rosenberg, and said they'd get worse than a brick next time. The police aren't much interested in finding out who did it; they're too busy arresting people for selling dime bags. My mother calls the police fucking fascists, and the skinny young man says, "You said it, sister." I ask my mother what a fascist is, and she says it's someone like Ronald Reagan, who doesn't want poor people to have a good time. She adds that the word "cunt" is very bad and I'm not to repeat it, especially around my grandparents. It will occur to me only years later that she made no similar edicts against the word "fucking."

The Yankees pitch a no-hitter against the Red Sox that day. I know this because there are tons of people on Mimi's rooftop, sunbathing and listening to the game. Although it's ninety-four degrees out, Mimi roasts kielbasa on her hibachi. We eat it on hot-dog rolls spread with spicy mustard. My mother and Mimi top theirs off with horseradish.

My mother coaxes me into trying a bite. It's so pungent it brings tears to my eyes. I spit it out and take a huge swig of Orange Crush. My mother laughs at me and says my palate is retarded. Mimi ruffles my hair and says she didn't like horseradish, either, when she was my age and it's the sort of thing one has to grow into.

My mother and Mimi drink an entire twelve-pack of Schlitz. By the time the fireworks start, they're both very drunk, but Mimi holds her booze better than my mother, who is laughing and slobbering all over the place. It's scary to see my mother lolling all over Mimi and telling her how much she loves her, but Mimi doesn't bat an eye. She loops one of my mother's arms around her shoulders and the other around mine and says, "Come on, kiddo, let's get your mom some bed." We haul my mother down the stairs to Mimi's studio and deposit her, face first, on the futon. My mother groans. Mimi apologizes, calls her "slugger," says it's time for beddy-bye, and tucks a sheet around her.

We make a nest of blankets and pillows on the floor, and Mimi asks if I want anything to eat or drink and if I want to play Mad Libs. She brings over a bag of Doritos and a pitcher of water, half of which she drinks herself, along with an aspirin and a Vitamin-C tablet. She says it'll help her hangover in the morning. I know the word; my mother used it last Christmas, when she got drunk on eggnog at my grandparents' and got into a huge fight with my grandmother about money. I ask why it will help, and she says she has no idea, but it does, and that's all she cares about.

Mimi lets me go first at Mad Libs. She asks for a female celebrity. I ask what a celebrity is, and she says it's a famous person. I say Ethel Rosenberg, and Mimi bursts out laughing. She asks me how in the name of God's green Earth have I heard of her. I tell her about the documentary and the photo at P.S. 122 and how someone threw a brick through P.S. 122's window. Mimi shakes her head and says the world is full of sick people. I tell her Ethel Rosenberg looks mean, and she chuckles and says, "I'd look mean, too, if I were locked up in jail, especially for something I didn't do." She crawls to her feet and staggers over to the bookcase and pulls out a book with a yellow cover. Mimi tells me the book was written by the Rosenbergs' sons. She shows me a picture of them when they were little. One of them has rings around his eyes, like I do. I wonder if Ethel scolded him for not getting enough sleep, like my mother does. I ask if they're dead like Julius and Ethel, and Mimi says, no, they live in a town in Massachusetts near where

95

she grew up. She turns the page to a picture of Julius and Ethel kissing in the back of a prison van. On the next page is a picture of the boys clapping their hands while a woman plays a guitar. Mimi says that's their adopted mom and that their adopted dad wrote a very famous song called "Strange Fruit." I've never heard of it. I complain that adults are always talking about very famous things that I've never heard of, and Mimi laughs and says, yeah, adults are weird like that.

Mimi walks us home the next day. My mother has a horrible headache and she throws up on the corner of First Avenue and 10th Street. A tough-looking guy with a tattoo calls my mother a dumb bitch. As soon as he's past us, Mimi flips him the bird. We drag my mother up the three flights and put her to bed. Mimi brings her some Lipton Cup-a-Soup and a wastebasket. Before she leaves, Mimi pulls the yellow Rosenberg book from her NPR tote bag and tells me I can borrow it for as long as I'd like. She gives me a big hug and kisses the top of my head and says my mother will be fine but if I run into any trouble, I know how to reach her.

I take a glass of milk, some off-brand Oreos, and the book out onto the fire escape. Even though I read at a sixth-grade level, the text bores me, and so I settle for looking at the pictures. I keep returning to the picture of Julius and Ethel kissing in the back of the prison van. A dreamy feeling, like the one I get when I look at my grandmother's *Gone With the Wind* poster, comes over me. I feel like I could at once go to sleep and run laps around the block. In the apartment, my mother retches again.

The summer drags on. My mother wants me to play with the neighborhood kids. She says it makes her look bad that I don't have any friends. I did have a friend once, a soft, shy Vietnamese girl, but her older brother chased me off their front stoop with a baseball bat. The other kids scare me with their feral, jocular energy. They play double Dutch and know all the words to Donna Summer's and Michael Jackson's hits. In my head, though, I join them, cavorting through the sprinklers at Tompkins Square Park, singing, *Bad girl, bad girl, such a naughty bad girl, beep beep, uh huh.* Sometimes the Rosenberg boys join me. Sometimes I imagine Ethel and Julius watching.

One afternoon, the super is painting Rust-Off on the fire escape and my mother is in a foul mood, so I take my Rosenberg book out on the front stoop. Two hard, skinny girls point at me and laugh. They ask

me what I'm reading. I don't answer. One of them commands me to look at her. I don't. Before I have time to think, she's grabbed my book out of my hand and tossed it to her friend. Hooting with laughter, they play keep-away with it for half a block before deciding I'm too pathetic to warrant any more of their time and throwing the book in my direction. One of them calls me a fat-assed, white bitch. My mother tells me unfortunately that's the sort of thing I'm going to have to expect being white in our neighborhood, and that things have been unequal for centuries and this is the universe's way of evening it out and so I mustn't get upset about it. Years later, when I tell this story, a professor will ask me if I heard them correctly and accuse me of being a racist.

In the bath at night, I repeat the word "bullshit" until I feel tough. I start imagining myself as ten feet tall and able to do backflips through flaming hoops as "Thriller" blares from ghetto blasters in the background. I dream about going back in time to save the Rosenbergs. I've seen *Perry Mason* at my grandparents' house, and I picture myself bellowing, like Perry does, at Roy Cohn until he cries and admits he lied and the Rosenbergs are set free. I can't quite bring myself to imagine Roy Cohn in the electric chair, though, so instead I put him in a tiny cell and make him live on bread and water. For good measure, I throw his buddy Ronald Reagan in there with him.

One day, I'm practicing menacing expressions in my mother's makeup mirror when she tells me to stop screwing around, she's trying to take a nap. I tell her I'm not making any noise, and she says she doesn't give a flying fuck, this is her room and if I don't like it, I can go to my own stifling little cubbyhole of a room and roast to death. I yell that I hate her and I wish she'd die in the electric chair like Julius and Ethel Rosenberg. She leaps from the bed and wallops me across the face. She grabs fistfuls of hair and knocks my head between them. She throws me on the bed and tries to strangle me and screams if I ever talk that way to her again, she'll throw me in the East River and let the sharks have at me. A stream of urine gushes down my right leg. She wallops me across the face again and tells me to go get changed, that only babies wet their pants. She shoves me through the door into my room and slams it shut. I throw myself across my little bed, soaked and heaving with sobs.

Later, my mother lets herself into my room. She tells me she's sorry. I tell her to go away. She repeats that she's sorry, and I tell her again to

go away and that I hate her. I flinch, expecting her to hit me again, but instead she bursts into tears and runs toward the kitchen. I can hear her dialing the phone and wonder if she's calling the police on me. She talks to whoever it is for a long time, in a low voice. After she hangs up, I can hear her open the fridge and pop open a beer. She turns on WQXR on the kitchen radio and draws a bath. I can hear her choking sobs over the sounds of Mahler and the running water. I fall asleep.

When I wake up, it's dark and my mother is sitting on the edge of my bed. She tries to brush a lock of hair from my forehead, but I wriggle away. She nods as if she expected that. She says she knows I hate her and she doesn't blame me and what happened today will never happen again, but I have to promise to do as I'm told when I'm told to do it. I turn away from her and mutter "bullshit" so softly that I don't think she can hear, but she does. She says that's about what she expected and leaves the room. For years after, I will wonder if that means that's what she expected from the situation or if that's what she expected from me. A therapist will ask me if it matters. It will be at least another five years before I have an answer to that question, and even then I won't be sure.

My mother is grumpy and drowsy for the next week or so, but she doesn't hit me or even yell very much, and, for my part, I do as I'm told. I bring her water and order us dinner from Leshko's Coffee Shop two blocks away, which we eat while watching *The MacNeil/Lehrer Report*. A car bomb in Lebanon kills thirty-three. AT&T workers go on strike. My mother says something about how we'll be screwed without a telephone, but she supports the workers' right to strike. Almost as an afterthought, she tells me to never cross a picket line. I ask what a picket line is and she says those are the people holding up signs, like when the transit workers went on strike when I was four. She says I must never cross a picket line because the workers are striking for a reason and to do so would be very rude. I ask what if I have to pee where they're picketing, and she snorts and says, "Go pee someplace else."

On the morning of August 11[th], my mother sits boltupright in bed just as I'm tiptoeing into the kitchen for breakfast. She puts her finger to her lips and asks me if I heard that. I ask her if she means the garbage truck outside and she says, no, the bells. She says the bells at the Church of St. Brigid, on Avenue B, must be working again. I don't hear any bells and I tell her so. She calls me "man" and says I just have to listen, there's music all around us. She tells me to hurry up and eat

and get dressed and we'll go over to the playground. We haven't been to the playground in months. I eat my Cheerios so fast, half of them fall on the floor. I can't find my sneakers, and my mother says that's cool, just put on my flip-flops.

My mother joins me on the swings at the playground. She challenges me to a race. I pump as hard as I can, but my mother pumps harder. I yell that's not fair, she's bigger than I am, and she laughs into the wind and yells back she's going to fly so high, she'll turn upside down. She jumps off, like she's told me a million times not to do, and skins her knees, but she doesn't seem to mind. She catches me when I swing low enough and pulls me over to the wall where the Rastafarians are selling pot and playing Bob Marley on a boom box the size of a suitcase. My mother sings, *Don't worry about a thing, 'cause every little thing's gonna be all right.* One of the Rastafarians offers her a blunt. To my horror, she takes a huge toke. I have never seen my mother smoke anything before, although later I will learn she had quite a Salem Light habit in college and that she kept everything else behind closed doors. I tell her she's going to get cancer, and the Rastafarian grins at me and says ganja doesn't cause cancer, that my mother will be fine. She hands the blunt back to the Rastafarian, tells him Jah is righteous, and pulls me along, half walking, half skipping.

We walk past homeless people, some of them with the same purple splotches on their faces as the guy from P.S. 122, and plop down next to a couple of old Ukrainian guys playing checkers. My mother tells me they were Freedom Fighters in World War II. They barely notice us until my mother stands up on the bench behind one of them and starts yelling about how someone called Brezhnev had the right idea. The old man stands up and says something like "corva" and takes a swing at her, but she ducks and laughs and calls him an old fart. A police officer ambles by and tells my mother to calm down and get off the sauce. My mother yells back that she's high on life and no motherfucking pig is going to tell her what she can and can't do. The police officer tells her to cut the crap and get down from the bench. The old men are yelling at my mother in Ukrainian and shaking their fists. By now a small crowd has gathered. In Tompkins Square Park, though, this is a Tuesday, and so they mostly point and laugh. The police officer climbs up on the bench next to my mother and tries to grab her wrist. She takes a swing at him, and he wrestles her to the ground and into a pair of handcuffs. My mother calls him a motherfucking pig again and tells

him to go fight real crime. The police officer kneels on her back and tells her she has the right to remain silent. He looks up and sees me crying hysterically and removes his knee.

Another police officer shows up and helps lift my mother up off the ground. Her face is streaked with dirt and gravel. She has a faraway look in her eyes and she's muttering something unintelligible. The second police asks me if I'm her daughter and if there's anyone I can call to come get me. I ask if they're taking my mother to jail, and he says, no, just to Bellevue, where they'll give her some nice medicine that will make her feel better. He says that last part like I'm four years old, and I hate him for it. I let him escort me out to Avenue A, though, and into a waiting squad car, because there isn't anything else I can do. The driver insists I sit in the front. He jokingly asks me if I want him to do the siren. I don't answer.

The car pulls up in front of a cubelike building, and my mother is hauled out of the back. I start to go with her, but the officer tells me to stay with him, that Bellevue is no place for children. I ask if my mother is going to be OK, and he says hopefully, in a few days. He asks me if I know Jesus. He says if I know Jesus I will have eternal life and I must make a promise to turn my soul over to him and get saved. I start crying hysterically all over again. The first officer, the one who arrested my mother, hears my screams and runs back to the car. He must know the driver's schtick because he tells him, not here, not now, and radioes his base to have someone call Mimi to come get me.

I won't find out all the details until years later, when I've moved back to New York for college and I join forces with Mimi to obtain my mother's records. My mother is dead by then, of a blood clot to the lungs when I was twelve. It turns out she was manic-depressive and had been taking Tofranil, which is mostly harmless in unipolar depressives but can seriously fuck up the bipolar, and that's why she went crazy that day. She spends a week at Bellevue and is then transported by special ambulance to a high-rent facility in Virginia, near my grandparents' home, which she's in and out of for the rest of her days. It turns out she's also schizoaffective and has borderline personality disorder. She's living in a group home one town over from my grandparents when she dies in her sleep. I never get a chance to ask her if she's learned the people with the purple splotches are not, in fact, contagious.

I'm transported to Virginia, too, in my grandfather's Lincoln Town Car, and when I arrive at their sprawling house I'm given a Cabbage Patch Kid and told I can eat as much ice cream as I want, until routine sets in and my grandmother begins to scold me for eating too much and for not being ladylike. As the years pass, this will morph into screaming fights about politics and sex. It breaks my heart in 1984 when I find out my grandparents are voting for Ronald Reagan. It further breaks my heart when they tell me they don't want me to keep in touch with Mimi, that she has too many unsuitable ideas. In college, after I've looked Mimi up—she's living in Park Slope then—I'll find out this was because when my grandparents were cleaning out my mother's apartment, they discovered the Rosenberg book, which had Mimi's nameplate plastered on the inside cover, in my bedroom.

In high school history class, I'll be told the Rosenbergs were guilty and got what they deserved. In college, I'll meet a guy whose grandparents knew Julius and Ethel in the Young Communists and commence to fucking him senseless. It's through him that I finally hear Billie Holliday sing "Strange Fruit." We'll weep together over its contents. I'll find out later he's been seeing someone else when I wind up in the school infirmary with crabs. On the forty-fifth anniversary of their execution, I'll turn on the TV and see that same picture of Julius and Ethel kissing and feel as dreamy and elated as I did when I was seven, even though I've kissed dozens of people by then.

I will never accept Jesus, nor, when evidence comes out to the contrary, will I ever fully accept the Rosenbergs were anything but innocent.

But I don't know any of that then. On that day, I know only that Mimi is coming for me, and when she gets here, she scoops me up in her arms and kisses me many times. I bury my head in her root-beer-colored curls and inhale her familiar scent, a mixture of cinnamon gum and bamboo. The policemen offer to drive us home, but Mimi says no, thank you, and hails us a cab to take us back to the East Village, where we'll eat pizza for dinner and play Mad Libs every night until my grandparents come to pick me up.

# MOONSHINE BLUES, WOOLFITT
## ST. LOUIS BLUES
WILLIAM

when Bessie sings *reeling and rocking, howling like a hound*

we listen to her on wax cylinder, on eight-track tape, on YouTube

when she's been on the road with the Florida Blossoms, with cake
    walkers and chair balancers, Butterbeans and Susie

when she sings *I'll pack my grip, make my getaway*

we can almost taste bootleg, white lighting, low wine

when it's too dry for corn, when everyone's on the killing floor

when Bessie Smith barrelhouses, when she ohs    oohs    hums

we hear about places we've longed for, she's been there, she's
    studied the maps

when planes bomb crowded cities, when the water blisters our lips

when she sings *Sister Green / done a shimmy you ain't never seen*

something in our souls comes loose, we flutter, we yell and clap

when the Klan comes to her tent, she shakes her fist and shouts,
    *you just pick up those sheets and run*

# LAMENTATION <span>MICHAEL MEYERHOFER</span> FROM THE PRODUCE AISLE

I can't get this damn bag open no matter
how hard I massage and claw its translucence,
an impatient lover standing before me
waiting to deposit an eggplant which, believe it
or not, is not a euphemism, and as I try,
I start thinking about that time a pretty woman
with a stage name asked me to unknot her
tube top, at least thirty men watching,
only it wouldn't loosen, the crowd got restless,
and as I fumbled, I started thinking about
Alexander the Great, how those wise men gave him
a knot more complicated than the tax code
and asked him to solve it, which he did
by cleaving it with his sword, only the bouncer
made me transfer my pocket knife to the car
and anyway, taking your clothes off
is one thing but who wants a guy holding a knife
to your back, even if he promises to be
careful, even if he promises to set you free?

# AUTOBIOGRAPHY <span style="font-size:smaller">TED LARDNER</span> WITH SOME COWS ON A ROAD IN MICHIGAN PASSING THROUGH IT

In the valley below an observatory on a high hill in lower Michigan.
The hill is called Peach Mountain; the cows—eight or nine.
We couldn't count definitively; it was very dark, and though
cows are generally huge and usually slow-moving,

up-close like that, sitting among them, we in our car, they in their
cow-ness, we all shoved slowly deeply onwards. In the road, we mingled
like planets, blind, crowded together, our paths from darkness
to darkness interlacing, and what light there was fell from the interchange

over the field. Black and deep, and their eyes deep,
and the white edges of their bodies a result of headlights,
and our words ("Look!" he said. "Cows!" she answered).
We were Perseid streaks in the night. The cows were giant letters

that swirled into Holstein colors then out, mooing and walking,
it doesn't matter how many, and they didn't mind how far
from the pasture down on Peach Mountain,
to the barn up at the end of the road.

Thick on that branch of that night sky we dangled like leaves.
The road is called North Territorial; a century oak there
held a century farm in its clutches. The moon, though, since the beginning,
flies over everything, erasing, erasing.

She thought she loved him; he thought he loved her, too.
At the end of the road, through huge blanks of sky
where the barn doors swing wide, the cows jumped, drifting by us
like the billboards on Route 23. Gauging distance is hard.

TED LARDNER

# LEAVING, RON RIEKKI FOR THE MILITARY

I was a Frankenstein
who thought I'd become

a Navy Seal. I lost sixty
pounds in boot camp,

the pneumonia gutting
a tundra in my chest.

I kissed fever all night
in the body of the barracks.

I remember leaving
for war. I told some

girls in a bar and they
looked at me like I was

diseased. I was,
I suppose. It's called

patriotism. Just look
around.

*Moon City Review*, a publication of Moon City Press, is housed in Missouri State University's Department of English. While *Moon City Review* publishes writers from across the country and throughout the world, we remember our origins as an in-house journal by annually publishing one poem and one piece of fiction written by Missouri State students and selected in an open competition.

Poet and novelist Alexandra Teague, an MSU alum, served as judge for this year's poetry competition. Teague is the author of two books of poetry, *Mortal Geography* and *The Wise and Foolish Builders*. Teague selected Brandon Henry's poem "Stand for New Anthem" as this year's first-prize winner. Teague remarks,

> "Stand for New Anthem" skillfully uses the layerings and divisions of the villanelle form to enact this difficult political and environmental moment in our "indivisible nation": suspending and playing with the distance between "examination" and "nation," and questioning (with wonderful wording) the "mute ampersand" of social response that so often follows crisis.

The poetry staff at MSU chose five finalists in all, and along with Henry, the finalists include the following students:

<div align="center">

Shannon Ashley
Anthony Isaac Bradly
Seth Dowler
Hannah Hickman

</div>

For the fiction competition, novelist and short story writer Anne Valente selected the winner. Valente's first book and short story collection, *By Light We Knew Our Names,* won the Dzanc Books Short Story Prize in 2014, while her second book, *Our Hearts Will Burn Us Down,* was released by Wiliam Morrow in 2016. Valente chose Breea Schutt for her entry "Story Consumption" as the winner. In describing her choice, Valente writes,

Detailing a mother's management of her young daughter's hunger for eating books, this story is an absolute delight. Inventive, imaginative, and beautifully rendered, "Story Consumption" draws the reader in from the first sentence. I couldn't put this story down.

The fiction staff chose seven students' work in all, and along with Schutt's story, the other six finalists include the following authors:

Kevin Davis
Abigail Eskew
Brad Henderson
John King
Kiah Mott
Robin Prantl

Both "Stand for New Anthem" and "Story Consumption" appear in the following pages. We are proud to present this work to you and for them to receive exposure in this format.

# STAND HENRY
## BRANDON FOR NEW ANTHEM

We could all use some examination
in how flags at half-mast now stand for "new anthem."
Reflecting on an indivisible nation,

the teleprompter reads *Call out for patience*,
while the live stream, the manswarm, the verdict in hand.
We could all use some examination,

while the fire whipped by yells engulfs the Shell station
and the acquittals, dismissals, our mute ampersand
reflect on an indivisible nation.

Undivided under billionaire Exxon freemason,
these boardwalks advance on contested oil sand.
We could all use some examination

in how pipes run through Flint's solubility equation,
where leaded, unleaded fuel disquiets demands
reflecting on an indivisible nation.

Firewater spray freezes Meskwaki relations.
*It's only natural. (Disaster.) Part of God's plan.*
We could all use some examination,
reflecting on an indivisible nation.

# STORY SCHUTT
## BREEA CONSUMPTION

Ainsley Laeser's daughter, Hallie Laeser, loved sunflowers, hated bad weather, and was nourished by stories—in a literal sense. It took a while for Ainsley to figure this out. She had tried feeding her daughter everything, anything: breast milk, formula, 2 percent, smashed carrots and peas. For too long, Hallie was only nourished by a feeding tube, but then the girl was old enough to toddle, and be curious about how things felt in the grasp of her tiny fingers. As Ainsley was reading her umpteenth book concerning babies and their nutritional needs, all while hooking her index finger around the hair tie holding her ponytail in place (a nervous habit she had always had), Hallie half stumbled, half crawled, to the lowest section of the living room bookshelf. She took hold of one of the book's spines, opened it to a random page, tore the page down the middle, and shoved the ripped paper into her mouth. In a panic, Ainsley threw aside the book she was reading, ready to fish the page out of Hallie. "Open up," she commanded, squeezing the little girl's cheeks until they puckered like a fish. "Open up for Momma, Hal. Please."

But the page was gone, dissolved by the saliva pooling on Hallie's tongue and on its way to being digested by a body starved for too long. The nourishment took effect immediately; Hallie's cheeks turned pink and healthy, her energy spiked—reflected in the widening of her eyes—and she puckered her lips on her own accord to form her first word: "More."

The last time Ainsley took her daughter to the pediatrician was to get the feeding tube removed. The doctor asked, "How did you get her to eat?"

Ainsley smiled, patting back Hallie's dark, thickening hair. "I found what she liked."

☾

It was an adjustment, like every case that deals with something outside societal norms. Ainsley had to create bizarre rules for her daughter, like "Never consume book pages while still at the bookstore." This particular regulation was first put into place when Hallie was three, after an incident where she consumed half a book about shapes in front of a group of gaping toddlers.

"But Momma, I didn't know we had to pay for the books first," Hallie said from her car seat as she picked at the rubber sole of her sandal. "When you got pizza at that one place, you gave the guy monies after you ate."

Ainsley was still blushing terribly, trying to keep both hands on the wheel, though her hand kept reaching to mess with her ponytail. She had been scolded by two mothers, who thought it absolutely absurd she'd let her daughter eat half a book and, if it had been their daughter, they'd take her to a specialist immediately.

"Books are different," Ainsley said, looking in her rearview mirror, back at her sunshiny girl; whose hair was beautiful, skin was glowing, and was fine, just fine, for goodness sake. No reason to see some specialist.

Hallie was wonderfully well mannered for someone her age—except for the first time she experienced a tornado watch, in which she threw herself on the floor and screamed, "I hate this! I hate this, I hate this—stop, already!" A child with a fear of storms was easy. There were actually books on that. All the parenting guides talked about distraction being "the key that unlocks a child from anxiety-forged manacles" (so to speak). They practiced yoga, worked puzzles, read and nibbled on stories. Distract, distract, distract, until the sun came out again.

Hallie picked up the phrases, "Yes, Mommy," and "OK, Mommy," quickly, and used them often when Ainsley instructed her to act a certain way. They had a system now. On Monday mornings, the two would travel to their local bookstore and Hallie would pick out a week's worth of books. Then, they'd take the books home and, before meals, Ainsley and Hallie would curl up on the couch, where Ainsley would read the stories aloud before feeding them to her daughter.

Not every book Ainsley and Hallie read together was particularly nourishing. Spooky stories about ghosts and goblins were fun and

kept Hallie on edge but made her tummy feel icky at night. She complained about reading history books because they were boring, but she developed sudden cravings for them. "I miss the aftertaste," Hallie said.

Books about gardening were always her favorite. They were visually and physically delicious.

"I'm gonna start a garden, Momma," Hallie said a few days after her fourth birthday.

"Yes you are, baby," Ainsley said, and the two created a tiny plot in their backyard where they planted baby's breath, azaleas, daisies, and sunflowers.

Hallie's fourth-ever Valentine's Day was the worst V-day of Ainsley's life, not because she lacked companionship, but because it marked the date their local bookstore decided to permanently close its doors. Ainsley squeezed Hallie's hand, trying to block out her girl's persistent questions of, "Why's the building dark, Momma? Are the books sleeping? Mom. Mom, do you think they are, Momma? Is Mr. Book-seller sleeping? Should we wake him up?"

But "Mr. Bookseller" was not sleeping. And Ainsley stood there, simply grasping her daughter's hand as the young girl's interrogation continued. They waited for "Mr. Bookseller" to show up. He never did.

Ainsley finally loosened her grasp of Hallie's hand and began messing with her ponytail. "C'mon, baby. You want to read some of Momma's old books?"

Ainsley owned a computer, but she only knew enough about it to conduct basic searches on the Internet. That evening, her basic search was, "Bookstores near me."

There were a few; the closest was a thirty-minute drive eastward. Ainsley did a more general search: "Bookstores in the US." She breathed when she saw several destinations pop-up on a digitalized map of America. Thirty minutes wasn't bad. They could always move if they had to. For now, she would learn how to order online—in case life got in the way and thirty minutes became too far.

March was always a difficult month for Hallie; it either came or left like a lion. This time, it was leaving, and a giant roar of thunder made

her press against her mother's side closer, closer still. She whimpered, even though Ainsley was trying to read her a book of nursery rhymes, which she always said were tasty, but never filling—a nice, afternoon snack.

Ainsley paused during "Little Boy Blue" and followed Hallie's gaze out the back patio window, where the rain came down in generous dollops; each drop gulped when landing against the pane.

"The flowers need the rain, Hal," Ainsley said. She could feel Hallie's bony shoulders slump with possible acceptance. They listened to the rain together. When Hallie finally fell asleep, Ainsley glared at the rain pattering the windows, silently challenging it to disrupt the safety of their living room. Don't you dare wake my baby, she wanted to say. Ainsley hoped the weather could read her mind.

She broke her stare to glance at the digital clock, resting on the highest tier of the living room bookshelf. The mailman hadn't arrived yet. Hopefully he'd be courteous enough to place her pending package on the front doormat, under the awning and out of the storm.

It didn't happen overnight. It was a slow transformation. Ainsley should've been more mindful when she saw pop-up ad after pop-up ad for the latest digital readers on her book sites. She remembered from when she was a child how trends shifted: cassettes to CDs to iTunes. VHSs to DVDs to Blue-rays. It was happening again, and everyone else seemed to treat the shift like its trendy predecessors—just another fad-train society was expected to ride. Ainsley only began to truly accept this shift as reality after Hallie asked for more books involving the Mouse who wanted milk to go with his cookie. When Ainsley searched for the series, she found the newest releases were available "on eBook only."

The swivel chair Ainsley sat in creaked slightly to the left, turning away from the screen, and she let it. She was trying to pull herself together, but messing with her hair tie wasn't enough. So she balled her fists against her eyes until white splotches appeared in her vision and breathed.

Distract, distract, distract.

Ainsley didn't listen to herself. She turned back to the computer screen and searched something she hadn't in a while: "Bookstores in the US."

113

The results made her call Hallie's pediatrician for the first time in three years.

"Hallie needs stories to survive," she blurted when the receptionist answered. The receptionist, bless her, attempted to make sense of—what Ainsley assumed sounded like hysterical jibberish from her end; eventually, her call was simply transferred to the pediatrician himself, Dr. Shiell.

"Stories," he muttered. Ainsley could mentally picture him stroking his beard as he pondered this. "And you need an alternative source of nourishment?"

"Please," Ainsley said.

"Hmm." Another pause. Ainsley grasped her cell phone tighter. "Have you considered alphabet soup?"

Ainsley thought back to when Hallie was two, when she, indeed, tried alphabet soup. Ainsley spelled out words like "dog" and "to" and "pot," but a can of alphabet soup only spelled out a handful of words. Books like *The Cat and the Hat* filled Hallie up. In order to recreate that same nutritious satisfaction with alphabet soup, Ainsley would have to purchase nine cans of soup per day, and spend the rest of her life spelling out noodle-stories for Hallie to consume. She could try, but it definitely wasn't a happily-ever-after scenario.

"There's gotta be another way," Ainsley said.

Dr. Shiell sighed, filling the receiver with a crackling thunder. "Ms. Laeser. Words are everywhere. You can write words, I can write words. I am currently looking at a whole slew of words on the back of my McDonald's cup: 'Download our app for exclusive deals, nutrition info, and more!'"

"I'm not going to feed my daughter a Styrofoam fast-food cup. She needs stories."

"All I'm saying is your daughter is not going to starve."

Ainsley continued to listen, but her grasp on the phone had loosened so drastically, it threatened to slip from her palm.

"In this ever-changing society," Dr. Shiell continued, "marketers just … they don't consider special cases like Hallie's. Everyone adapts. But, that doesn't mean your little girl's going to starve. She's just going to have to learn to be less picky with what she eats. And you're going to have to be less picky about what you feed her. Do you understand, Ms. Laeser?"

Of course she understood. That's what was scaring her.

☾

"Momma," Hallie said the day after Ainsley's phone call with Dr. Shiell. The little girl was sitting on the dryer, kicking her little heels against it.

"Don't kick the dryer, baby," Ainsley said absently, throwing the whites into the dryer's maw.

"Momma, my daisies are dying."

"They'll come back."

"Why do the daisies next door stay alive?"

"What, Ms. Mae's flowers? They're fake, Hal."

"Fake?"

"Yeah, they're plastic. She doesn't have to do anything to them. They just exist."

"Can I have daisies like that?"

Ainsley slammed the dryer with more oomph than she wanted. It probably did more damage than Hallie's little heels would have. "What about your garden?"

"I can't have a garden and fake flowers, too?"

"Which would you prefer?"

Hallie lifted her feet, pulling back for another kick, then thought better of it when she saw Ainsley's eyebrow-arch warning. "I dunno. I just like flowers. All kinds of flowers. Reds and yellows and blues …."

For the next several months, Ainsley tried something new: printing. She would find stories online she figured Hallie would enjoy and print them for breakfast. Initially, it was a beautiful solution. The words were still tangible, the stories still readable. Sometimes, Ainsley even typed her own, which Hallie enjoyed—especially when the protagonists of the short tales just so happened to, also, love flowers and hate storms. However, ink was expensive, and the tax on paper increased with seemingly every trip Ainsley took to the store, and notebooks were starting to be considered "cool" and "vintage" by hipster teens.

The inflation of such commodities was not kind to Ainsley's already-sparse bank account. After her last trip, when her total rang up to an absurdly high price, she demanded to speak with the manager. It was a lost cause, and she knew that before the beefy woman with the gold name tag introduced herself and asked, "What seems to be

the problem?" But that didn't stop Ainsley from being one of those customers, the ones she used to personally condemn.

"When I was growing up, the combined price of ink and paper did not equal the price of a brand-new printer."

"I understand your concern, ma'am. It's an environmental tax. Save the trees and whatnot."

"You wanna save the trees? Stop building log houses. Or ban bonfires."

"I'm sorry, ma'am, I have no control over the prices at this store. May I recommend one of the tablets in our electronics section? You pay around the same price you just spent, but it's only a one-time cost. And you can download all your documents in as many folders as you li—."

Ainsley stormed out the automatic doors. She knew the employees would talk, and call her the crazy lady who yanks at her ponytail and takes her issues out on people who really don't have a say on pricing issues—Oh, what a sad, sad individual Ainsley Laeser must be! She has nothing better to do than complain about products no one cares about buying anymore.

Hallie would be attending preschool soon. Ainsley knew she couldn't keep her away from other kiddos any longer, but that didn't keep her from countless restless nights. Hallie would starve. She'd have to stare at videos of other people reading stories, and her stomach would growl and groan. She'd want to rip the pages and shove them in her poor little mouth—to taste them, to make them tangible—but they would always be out of her reach, and none of the kids would understand her hunger.

Thunder rumbled outside. Ainsley had been lost in thought again. She did that often nowadays, just as often as she checked online to see if any more bookstore closings had happened. She checked for libraries, too, which always made her feel significantly better. If need be, later on through the years, she could always feed Hallie with the books in their circulation. Sure, they would need sterilized from being touched by so many and, yes, she would owe quite a large fine from damaged and missing books, but surely the librarians would understand. Her baby needed these.

Still, the selfishness of her idea stung. She would be nurturing her own child and depriving future children from what could be, potentially,

one of the few, remaining hard copies of whatever books Hallie chose to consume.

More thunder rattled the windows. The rain started to come down in sheets.

"Hal, what story do you want for supper?" Ainsley called out, brewing a pot of decaf for herself in the kitchen. She poured a mugful, then stirred in a scoop of sugar.

Hallie hadn't replied. Ainsley stopped stirring. There was a good possibility Hallie was hiding in her closet, waiting for the storm to pass. It was her newest distraction—blocking out the noise entirely. "Hal, did you hear me?"

Ainsley grabbed the coffee and let it heat her hands as she shuffled down the hall to Hallie's room.

"Hal?"

She creaked the door open with her elbow. Hallie's room was dark, and she hadn't made her bed like Ainsley requested, but Ainsley's irritation was dulled by the familiar lump that revisited her throat time and again—a lump that appeared when she noticed Hallie's bookshelf, and how its shelf space was less filled with books and more filled with artificial flowers found at the grocery store for a dollar, or with Ms. Mae's "daisies" she had given Hallie to "keep safe." Hallie owned so many now. They didn't need rainstorms or sunlight; they simply existed.

"Hal?" Ainsley called out again. She opened the girl's closet. Shirts dangled from hangers and shoes were piled in the corner, but there was no Hallie.

Ainsley set her coffee mug on Hallie's desk a little too forcefully; the contents sloshed out of their cup. "Hallie!"

She searched every room. Hallie wasn't under Ainsley's bed, peeking past the dust ruffle like she'd done before during games of hide-and-seek. She wasn't in the bathroom trying to start her own bubble bath, or in the laundry room trying to climb on top of the washing machine. And though she wasn't doing any of those things, Ainsley kept thinking about when Hallie had done them, because sometimes Ainsley found her life flashing before her eyes without the threat of death knocking at her own door.

"Hallie, baby? Come out, please? Come out for Momma, baby. Please. Please, don't do this."

And then Ainsley caught movement out of the corner of her eye. Past the patio window. Outside. In the rain.

Ainsley sprinted across the living room and slammed the sliding glass door open.

There Hallie sat, atop the soil where her garden once thrived. She sat with an umbrella, which canopied over herself and a single, remaining sunflower. She sat in the middle of a storm that, Ainsley knew, scared her.

"Baby," Ainsley said, but her soft words were washed away with the rain. She spoke up: "What're you doing out here?"

Hallie responded, but Ainsley couldn't hear her over the storm. The sunflower's petals swished against the material of the umbrella as a gust of wind riffled both it and Hallie's hair.

Ainsley thought about praising Hallie for her bravery, but what was this girl trying to prove? She didn't have to prove she wasn't afraid this way. She could've stayed inside and watched the rain come down, dry and safe.

Ainsley reached for her ponytail, but the hair tie snapped. Her hair draped against her shoulders in dark, wet, unfamiliar strands.

"Can Momma bring supper out to you?" Ainsley asked, mindlessly twisting the broken tie around her index finger.

Hallie looked up. She nodded once.

So Ainsley tucked her own, worn copy of Charlotte's Web under her cardigan and ran back outside, back under the umbrella that, surprisingly, protected them all quite nicely for the time being.

# GREAT-GRANDMOTHER BULLIS

## JENNIFER IN THE WOODS (GROSSOTO, LOMBARDY, C.1902)

on foot through the woods to the border
two days and one night to the *svizzero* side
to the hotels on the mountain
a hotel is a job          a job is a meal          is a roof
a hotel is a broom and a mop and a cloth

the other girls from my village walk together
our mothers warn us
only puttanas go into il bosce alone
but if I arrive before the others
the kitchen may begrudge me breakfast

home is a door with no lock
a job is a coin and a lump of hard cheese in my pocket
the woods are a bridge and a hole in the bridge
the woods are the night
                    the woods are a gap in the night

# GRANDMOTHER <small>BULLIS</small>
## <small>JENNIFER</small> IN THE WOODS
## (WASHOE VALLEY, NEVADA,
## C. 1920)

the woods are a gap in the heat
      ponderosa      juniper

just above the fields at the edge of the valley
      dust        flies

so much work in the heat
      mops      dishes      hoeing      milking

I asked to rest like my brother
Mother said when my work is finished

I asked to study like my brother
Mother said my schooling is finished

I escaped to the woods
Mother said only puttanas go into il bosce alone

I was alone until
my uncles followed me there

home from the war

they taught me what they learned in the war

the woods are a gap in the day
and a hole in the cage

      fir        lodgepole
the woods are a hole in the earth and my foot in the trap

# LANDSCAPE <span>BULLIS</span> WITH SUPPLICATION
## JENNIFER AND ART SUPPLIES

Anything can happen in the woods. I am one
of the women who goes alone, in spite of everything.
I'm aware of the drawbacks. I pack my fears

and my paint kit. The problem with watercolors
is they're transparent. The problem with gouache
is it's opaque. You can look without seeing, or see

without looking. The woods are good for both:
hiding and discovering. Revealing and obfuscating.
The medicine woman at the gallery showed me

her porcupine-quill beads and her bison-hide drum,
and exclaimed to my weeping, *Ah! You're one
of the migrators. You can send your healing directly,*

*you know.* No, I didn't know. But I am one
of the askers, so I asked permission, and did.
Knelt at the stream, poured water from one hand

to the other, praying for my mothers: *Healing
to her heart, comfort for her loss. Healing to her body,
balm for her spirit.* Water hand to hand, falling back

to the creek. Don't know what printed out
at the other end. The problem with ink
is it runs under teardrops. To console my heart,

I painted firs and cedars in acrylics.
The problem with acrylics is controlling
the drying. The problem with oils is controlling

the fumes. *Healing to my knees, balm
for my spirit.* Pouring water at the stream,
hand to hand to hand. *Comfort for my loss,*

*healing to my heart.* A cost, an art. I am aware
of the drawbacks. I am one of the ones the wind
blows through.

# THE FIGHT WRIGHT
## KIRBY OF THE CENTURY

The fight between Muhammad Ali and Joe Frazier was scheduled for March 8th in my sophomore year, the day before my mother's birthday. Promoters had dubbed their match "The Fight of the Century" because both fighters were undefeated. Ali predicted a KO in Round 6. Many fans believed Ali should never have been stripped of his title. The Vietnam War had fragmented the country, and Ali's resistance was considered courageous by some but cowardly by others. My father believed Ali was hiding behind religion.

I was rooting for Frazier. He was the underdog, and I admired his courage challenging a bigger man.

My father came home early on the day of the big fight. He flashed three tickets and announced, "The men in the family are going to the fight." He phoned the Ranch House and made reservations for our post-fight dinner.

June Spoon put on her fake smile, the one where she didn't show her teeth. She said she'd make due with a fried chicken TV dinner while Jenny ate spaghetti out of a can. Staying home always bummed her out because she loved dressing up and gracing locals with her presence. My mother's wit and charm had made her a bit of a celebrity at the Ranch House.

My brother trailed after me out to the Olds, where I squeezed in back. Troy rode shotgun. Dadio backed out while Troy fiddled with the radio. June Spoon stood in the dining room with her arms crossed.

Dadio handed Troy our tickets and he scouted the Honolulu International Center. The auditorium was oval shaped with a cement floor and a phalanx of hydraulic doors. It smelled of popcorn, cigarettes,

and pakalolo. The smoke clung to the rafters like fog. Prelim boxers were duking it out on a jumbo screen mounted beneath the ceiling.

Troy found our seats and I hunkered down between him and our father.

The HIC buzzed with gossip. Burly men in orange Terminix shirts guzzled from red cups. Boys gobbled hot dogs and wolfed down popcorn. A chant of "Ali, Ali, Ali" circled the arena.

"Can Frazier do it?" I asked my father.

"He's gotta take the fight to Ali," he replied, itching his nose. "Frazier's gotta get inside that long reach of his. Our guy's the slugger and Ali's the boxer."

"Were you a slugger?"

"I was a boxer."

"Like Ali?"

"Sort of. But I didn't dance."

"I'll buy us hot dogs," Troy volunteered.

"No hot dogs," Dadio replied. "We're going to the Ranch House."

"Even if Ali wins?" I asked.

"Yes. Even if he wins."

"How 'bout some popcorn?" Troy pressed.

"That crap fills you up even more than a hot dog."

It was time for the main event. Ali, dressed in a crimson robe, made his way through the Madison Square Garden mob. The Honolulu fans hooted and hollered. Ali ducked through the ropes. Angelo Dundee, his trainer, removed his robe. Ali wore red trunks trimmed with white.

Dadio stuck a hand in his pocket and jiggled his coins. "Here we go, boys," he said, "here we go."

I took a deep breath and fired a jab over the head of the man in front of me. I faked a hook to Dadio's belly. He grunted. Sometimes we did fake boxing at home, where I threw a slow left and he countered with a lazy right. I was two inches shorter than him. My brother was three inches taller than Dadio. Troy didn't seem related to us because of his blond hair. He'd frown whenever our father praised me for getting good grades. He couldn't stand me. But I wasn't alone. He'd demoted Chuck Marsland from best friend to acquaintance after Chuck made the volleyball team. With Troy, you started out with 100 points. Deductions soon followed, eventually reducing you to a sworn enemy.

A crescendo of boos welcomed Joe Frazier as he made his way to the ring. He slipped through the ropes in green trunks trimmed in yellow. His thighs were heavy with muscle and his biceps popped. Frazier wore a defiant look. Both fighters wore white boxing shoes but Ali's had red laces. They met in the middle of the ring for instructions from the ref. Ali glared down at his opponent. Frazier's eyes said he'd do his talking with fists. The ref warned about mandatory eight counts and neutral corners in case of a knockdown.

Troy elbowed me. "Ali" in six."

"Guess again," I said.

"Bet?"

The bell rang. Ali flicked his long left while Frazier bobbed and weaved. Ali connected with a lead left and followed that up with an overhand right. Joe kept coming. A right uppercut to the jaw wobbled Frazier. I prayed for Joe to go the distance. Even if he lost, I would still consider it a victory if he hurt Ali. The fighters made me think of Rock 'Em Sock 'Em Robots, those toy robots that knock off each other's blocks. A lightning-fast left snapped Frazier's head back. Frazier smiled through his mouthpiece. The bell ended the round. Burt Lancaster and Archie Moore were the ringside commentators and they discussed Round 1 as highlights played in slow motion. An overhand right whacked Frazier's face and a right hook slammed into Ali's belly. "Frazier is really unrelenting," Lancaster said.

"How can Frazier keep coming like that?" I asked.

"He's determined," Dadio said.

Determination had shaped my father as a boy. His drive to excel in school was motivated by the fear of turning out like his uncles, men who earned meager wages training boxers at CYO Gym. As a teen, my father had planned to fight his way out of the slums and begged his uncles to train him. After a few lessons, Sharkey put him in the ring with a pro. Fearless Frankie pounded him mercilessly for three rounds, cracking two ribs and splitting an eye so badly it needed a dozen stitches. But it had taken courage for a kid to hang in there with a ranked middleweight.

The bell sounded for Round 2. Ali came out dancing and Frazier took five shots before landing a hook. But it was a good punch and it backed Ali up.

"Frazier's gutsy," I said.

Troy smirked. "More guts than brains."

Frazier didn't go down after a flurry of brutal combinations. He even dominated Round 6, the round Ali predicted he'd fall. "Joe's just murder in there," said Burt Lancaster. "He's one of the toughest men you'll ever see." Ali stood flatfooted against the ropes as Frazier unleashed a barrage of body blows. The Fight of the Century was a grueling display of punishment, an epic battle waged between two black men born and raised in the South. Ali looked like a big brother toying with a younger sibling when he bombed Frazier with long-distance shots. An "Ali, Ali, Ali" chant resonated through the Garden and Round 7 ended. Ali raised his arms like a victorious gladiator.

During Round 8, Ali leaned against the ropes while Joe hammered away. A "Joe, Joe, Joe" chant went up in the HIC.

I popped up. "Joe, Joe, Joe!"

My father joined me.

Troy remained in his seat.

The bell ended the round but I refused to sit. So did my father.

"Frazier's a little man," Lancaster said, "but he's like a Sherman tank."

Seven rounds remained. Dadio seemed to shrink beside me, as if some of the air that kept him inflated had leaked out. He'd sunken into his familiar slouch. It was difficult believing that body had beaten us most of our lives.

Round 9 began. Ali smashed Frazier with left-right combos and uppercuts. Frazier's face was a mess of welts but his legs looked as strong as iron. A pulverizing right to the forehead halted his advance and fans muttered a collective "uggh."

Dadio shook his head. "Our man's pau."

But Frazier survived Rounds 9 and 10. In Round 11, he cornered Ali against the ropes and nailed him with a left hook to the jaw. Ali stumbled around the ring with Frazier in hot pursuit.

"Knock dat bum out!" Dadio called.

Frazier threw a wild left. The boxers clinched. The bell rang and Ali staggered back to his corner. "Frazier really clobbered his man," said Lancaster. "He hit him with everything in the book." Dundee screamed at Ali but there was a look of resignation in his fighter's face.

"Round twelve is the end," my father predicted.

"It'll go the distance," Troy countered.

Dadio cleared his throat. "Not a chance. Ali's dead on his feet."

Ali surprised my father by making it through Round 12. The

closing rounds were mostly clinches. In Round 15, Joe unleashed a wicked hook that found his rival's jaw. Ali dropped. I hugged my father. He hugged me back. Ali took the mandatory eight. I'd wanted him to lose but still felt bad seeing him like this. He was human after all and could get clobbered like anyone. Frazier couldn't finish the job but, when the final bell rang, everyone knew Joe had pulled the upset. Cops in Madison Square Garden struggled to restore order in a ring mobbed by sportswriters, fans, and bodyguards. Burt Lancaster said Frazier had slumped down in his corner. Dundee unlaced his fighter's gloves. Ali lowered his eyes when the announcer read the scores giving Frazier the victory.

It was nine when we arrived at the Ranch House, a family-style eatery in Aina Haina. The Wild West theme featured a life-size wooden Apache with a hatchet glaring beside the register.

"Good evening, Mister Wright," the redheaded hostess greeted.

"Hello, Shirley," Dadio said. "Good to see you."

Waitresses in petticoats zipped by carrying trays filled with steaks, ranch fries, soup, and baked potatoes. The aroma of grilled meat made me hungry. Murals of cowboys were painted on the beige stucco walls, everything from cowpokes driving cattle over the Rio Grande to broncobusters getting tossed into the sky by mustangs. Cowhides, bridles, and stirrups hung off hickory posts. The décor included round tables with checkered red-and-white tablecloths, kerosene lanterns, and vases filled with breadsticks. A longhorn's head was mounted above the saloon doors. The only thing not Wild West was a fish tank opposite the Apache.

Mr. Spencer, the bald manager, led us to a table beside a mural of a cowboy branding a calf. I sat between my father and brother. My father called the manager "Spence." Spence always flirted with my mother and was disappointed she wasn't with us. Dadio said we'd come from "the big fight." Spence nodded. He told my father riding Brahma bulls was "far more challenging than fighting with pillows on your hands." Shirley whispered something in Spence's ear and they both took off.

I gushed about the fight like a kid whose football team had defeated a favored rival. Troy offered me a fake smile. I was sure he identified with the rebel in Ali and considered me an Uncle Tom like Frazier, a sellout who'd fritter away his life trying to please our father. Troy performed his "float like a butterfly, sting like a bee" impersonation of

Ali. Dadio chuckled, saying he sounded just like him. I threw a slo-mo punch that tapped my brother's jaw. He slumped over. Our father was pleased in the warm surroundings of the Ranch House and I knew Frazier's victory had restored order to his universe. He believed people got what they deserved in life and, in his mind, Ali's draft-dodging past had caught up with him.

A blond girl in a buckskin mini served my father his martini, and we all followed her with our eyes as she bounced back to the saloon. The waitress arrived. Dadio insisted we each eat a porterhouse steak instead of him ordering the usual plank steak and him dividing it up. The waitress nodded and split.

You know," Dadio told us, "when you were little boys, we had to reserve the table beside that big tank so you could watch the fish. Otherwise, you'd be chasing each another all over this restaurant and screaming outside at the monkeys."

"Saint Vitus Dance," I joked.

"We called you the Niki Hoeky Boys. What one didn't think of, the other one did."

"Did we get invited back to parties?" I asked.

"Not once. I remember you dunking the birthday boy's head while Troy swan-dived off the roof into their pool."

"Just goin' it," my brother said.

"After dinner," Dadio continued, "we'd stroll to that big park where McDonald's is now and you'd both go, 'Nah, nah, nah, nah, nah, nah,' teasing me to chase you."

"Did you catch us?" I asked.

"A few times. But remember, that was after a big meal and a coupla drinks and there were no lights in that park. I'm lucky I didn't fall into a hole and bust my ankle."

I loved it when our father told family stories I'd heard countless times. It was as if an old record were playing, and I remembered the good things we shared.

Troy snapped a breadstick. "Remember the monkeys?"

"I sure do," Dadio replied, "in that big cage out back. Spence got rid of 'em all when that big male bit the owner."

"Did he get rabies?" I asked.

"I don't remember anything about that. Monkeys are, by their nature, very aggressive. They bite for no reason at all."

"Maybe the owner teased it," Troy suggested.

Our father gulped his martini. "Well," he said, "if he did tease that monkey, he got what was coming."

It felt good being with my father. His mind wasn't churning over legal problems and he wasn't hunting down broken things to fix at home. His sons had become, if only for this night, the closest thing to friends he had. He praised our waitress for being attentive and told Spence at the register to pay his compliments to the chef. I understood what my mother had seen in him back in Boston. He was the dashing major who offered her a lifetime in paradise.

Troy and I strolled the parking lot with our father between us. Our strides matched as we marched the blacktop. The moon lit up the white top of the Ranch House's covered wagon.

"Chase us," I said to my father, "for old-time's sake."

"Yeah," said Troy. "A strip of that old park's still left."

"You boys are too fast for me now."

We pulled out of the lot and I knew our father was happy spending time with us. He'd admitted to me he had no friends because of work demands but the real reason went deeper. He had been suspicious of people and their motives since his hanai days in Kaimuki. He drove up Kalanianaole Highway and passed Star of the Sea. We were minutes from his old stomping grounds, a town that had left an indelible mark with its daily doses of cruelty and shame.

We cruised through Kahala. I wondered if the good feelings between my father and me would be there in the morning or even make it through the night. He rolled into the driveway and pulled up to our dark house.

# TRANSLATIONS FROM CHILDHOOD

NAOMI RUTH LOWINSKY

There is a line on the inside of a bent knee
This caused my brothers to explode
with laughter     I never knew

what this was code for
since "African Jungle" was their name
for our mother's dark

underbrush     out of which it was said
we'd emerged     My brothers snickered
my father's voice rose

*Potfadorry! Jetzt hab ich aber eine Wut!*

I tried to stay above this
talking Adlai Stevenson
buttermilk dressing

putting my sorry body
my agony eyes between
my father's hands   my brothers'

provocations     Did that prevent him
from knocking their heads together
from giving each an *Ohr Feige?*

I never learned what
*Potfadorry* means     Perhaps
it is a warrior call to rouse

the blood     I know that *Wut*
is hotter and nastier
than anger     I know an *Ohr Feige*

is an ear fig   to avoid it   I hid
behind a fig leaf   and watched
                    that serpent raise     his head

NAOMI RUTH LOWINSKY

# MATRIARCH

One Saturday years before I was born,
my father who'd failed law school
fell to the kitchen floor. Grandmother,
a nurse, stood beside him, while my sister
hid behind the table, a witness
in clove-stuck air. It takes
a certain kind of woman to keep
shucking husks, distract the child
with the art of pulling silk from tight
yellow teeth, scrape the cobs
with a dull knife, butter and salt
the milky kernels just right.

Anyone can show up late
and drunk at the screen door,
anyone can scream
his daughter's name,
and when she decrees,
*No, you're not taking her,*
anyone can bang the door wide,
enter a blackout of his brain's rage.

But it takes a certain kind
to cast about for the closest weapon,
to deliver the blow, a verdict laid out
on a linoleum sea with a rose motif,
blooms the size of festooned cabbages.

# MATRIARCH

Order held high in our maternal
grandmother's hand, sure and tight
as if wrapped around a gavel. The iron
skillet fell, slow to fast, pounding once.
Only a pause to check the guilty's pulse.
*He'll live.* Order among the sink and stove,
among roiling beans steaming the afternoon.

JO BRACHMAN

# THE LAKE PEOPLE

GABRIEL WELSCH

In the marina float
American flags humid
as the creaking roof
of the ancient pavilion.

Two loungers talk and recall
great landforms they didn't see—
a fog-bedded Grand Canyon,
Great Salt Lake in starless dark.

Thunder rolls like moving on,
soft slap of a motorboat wake
frowning its way to the docks,
rusty call of gulls.

For those who sit here
every year, the summer plods glacial
and the continent beneath drifts
faster than any headline suggests.

# I'M SAILING AWAY

WYATT MCMURRY

When the violinist opens with a cover
of Styx's "Come Sail Away" I look

for the door, but the crowd's too thick,
the exits stuck off in a corner by the bar,

so I resign myself—and there, somehow,
seventh grade freezing upwells like a gust

of water .... I remember after Mr. Donovan
relented, Nick wrote his final paper

on Styx's 1977 hit. His thesis still sticks
like a barnacle to my skull: *This song*

*by Styx shows the emotion of the ocean.*
The rhyme really made it, and Nick, knowing

his strong suit, milked it for every pearl—
*The ocean's emotional potion, like a lotion,*

*an ocean full of emotional notions.* How right
he was, I thought, listing along against

my will with the slant-lit kelp forest
the disco ball plunged me into. How strange

that Nick, as if ankle deep in some tidal
pool and loving it, would later accept

Dennis DeYoung's invitation to set course
by misting his tongue with a spritz of liquid

Xanax. And the lampshades are singing
*come sail away*, and the car alarms are gurgling

*come sail away*, and the garden of bean pods
behind his mother's garage is demanding *water*

*water everywhere* slushes on the old tune,
and I wish I could say I only

imagined what it was like to float up into deletion
like a body that fills with gas and won't stay

down, but I too held hands with Nick and drowned
for minutes at a time, veins fattening with gasps

of song, that musical bends I left
to take him alone in the scoured-out wreckage

of Lexington Avenue. I almost wish I could
think filling my lungs as deep with the water

I helped lead him to would mean I'd been
a better friend. But I stayed shin deep.

I watched his body sink. And maybe
that was the right thing to do.

# BUTTER TROY
## MARY CAKES

I was on a driverless Greyhound bus in a Walmart parking lot in Yuma, Arizona, because Roger'd given me breast enlargement surgery for my forty-second birthday, because Dad had won a fake gold medal from the lepers, and because Not-Becky loved a lettuce picker. I said it to myself that way and laughed out loud, alone on the bus except for Dad. I knew others—Roger, Trevor, maybe even my addict mother—would tell me the situation wasn't funny. The sun in this strange land rose fast from behind the Walmart that cloudless September morning, baking Dad and me so thoroughly in our bus-turned-oven, we likely were not even red at the bone. And though preteen boys in white tees and low-slung jean shorts circled us on their bikes four times, banging on the back of the bus with each pass, Dad slept beside me, Row 11, Seat B, drooling and sputtering, a thick shock of pure-white hair shading an eye. I worried that when reality smacked him hard and what he already knew was proven, we'd have to confront his confusion and yearning. But until then, I added to my list of causality. We were stuck on this hot bus because my brothers/cousins thought I was a bad driver, because Dad made butter cakes, and because Doctor Duckworth proved to be the quack his name suggested.

Three weeks earlier, Roger's well-fed face glowed when he gave me my birthday gift a week before my birthday. He said he couldn't wait. "Boobs!" he said. "Yours are great, Gracie, but they can be even better." A few days later, a plastic surgeon with a face like a wedge of white cheddar squeezed and poked and giggled and said Cs would work best with my frame. Even so, Roger tried to sell Ds, wanted her to say Ds were possible, the more natural-looking, teardrop-shaped ones,

too. "You're still good-looking, Gracie," he said. "Why go through the rest of your life not being totally hot?"

I awoke on my actual birthday alone, Roger having left quietly for work hours earlier, a niceness in him since the third round of university budget cuts had finally cut me. I wanted to get up and dressed and was making a list of reasons to do just that, the only thing on it so far the fat but misshapen Big Boy tomato from my neighbor's garden sitting on the kitchen table. Then Dad called and said, "Gracie, my girl, want to go to Molokai?"

In Dad's kitchen later, I dug into his favorite lunch of extra-hot canned chili washed down with a vodka tonic. Dad pushed the ceramic chicken and rooster salt and pepper shakers aside to place a letter beside my bowl. The paper was thick and cream-colored with a gold, embossed royal palm tree in the upper right, its trunk trailing down the right side. The Association for the Advancement and Recognition of Kindness was pleased to present Dad with its gold medal. He would be honored at the awards dinner in Kalaupapa, Molokai. He smirked as I read it. "Some joker," he said. "I know lots of 'em." My brothers/cousins had already proven it was a hoax, Dad said, but he'd known from the first. Kirk went to the trouble of calling the not-working number, looking the fake association up online. "Doesn't exist. Still, I want to go," he said. "The prankster has given me a good idea. Haven't you always wanted to go to the leper colony?"

Dad wasn't the father I was born with but was my real mother's uncle and the family member who took me in before I was two because other family members ganged up on him. "Lost the coin toss," he said. "Drew the short straw." He laughed when he said it that way. The reason I needed replacement parents was a typical story about addicts turned into the kind of bums who make teary promises they can't keep. Dad said my real mother, even as young as fourteen, three years before she conceived me, was stealing radios and tape players from parked cars, selling them for drug money. She once broke into an unmarked police car and when arrested said she hadn't wanted to steal the radio but had heard a song as she walked by and was trying to turn the radio off to save the car's battery. "She's now living out West, selling insurance," was what he and the rest of the family said of her, what I learned early on was our family's version of saying the dog'd been sent to a farm in the country. We all thought she was likely dead.

Two years after Ralph and his wife Carol made me theirs, they had twins, my brothers/cousins, Kirk and Ken. Five years after that, Carol raced a Burlington Northern to a crossing and lost. People whispered at the time, wondering if Carol was unhappy and could it have been suicide, but Dad made us remember her explosive laugh, so loud she'd been asked to tone it down in more than one restaurant. And yes, it was stupid, but she'd often raced trains. Dad told us not to waste time being sad but to think instead of the joy she felt all those times she won. Which was every time, he explained. Until she didn't.

Roger shook his head and then scratched it when I told him no thanks on new breasts, said I'd rather take the money. I felt my face relax as I watched his sincere confusion, though his saying I was good-looking had pleased and surprised me, all brown cowlicks on top of a sweet-potato-like body. He said he knew I worried about my looks because he'd seen me staring into the mirror and frowning. He said again my B's were great, but wasn't bigger always better? He cupped his hands in front of his chest as he asked. He would've spent thirty-three hundred for the implants, the top-of-the-line silicone gel that was much more expensive than saline, but if I wanted money instead, he'd cut that in half. Once again, he shook his head, then scratched it. It was a habit I found oddly cute, miming his statements. His gestures now were meant to demonstrate confusion. "Your dad and the leper colony over bigger boobs for the rest of your life? Really?" He shook and scratched his head a third time. Eventually, he decided he should deduct the cost of the initial consultation too, which was $450.

Though I could have added my own money to the amount, and Dad could have as well, I suddenly wanted the trip to Molokai to be Roger's birthday gift, a trip to the leper colony for my forty-second from my soon-to-be-ex-whatever-he-was. I wanted to get there with Dad, stay in some sort of comfort, and get back for twelve hundred dollars.

I didn't know why I'd spent three years with Roger, the Associate Dean of Students at the small Christian college in St. Louis I used to work for. Sex, companionship, less time alone—those were all true, but, as with the others, not enough. I first spoke to Roger when he gave a talk on integrity in college admissions, and while chatting me up at the wine-and-cheese reception after, told me I had integrity coming out of my pores. He ran a hand down an arm when he said it

to show integrity flowing like water from his upper arm to his fingers. The action confused me, as I was supposed to be the one with integrity flowing. More than that, I'd not said anything that would scream out or even whisper integrity to him. As an admissions counselor I'd had to attend his entirely unmemorable lecture and PowerPoint, and my joke to myself was that real integrity would demand we told our new students they were entering a mediocre institution. It had kept me smiling throughout. Still, I liked his apple-pie face.

At the family meeting about how Dad and I would get to Molokai for twelve hundred and pay for hotels and meals, we four sat around the kitchen table, and Ken and Kirk laughed more at the fancy-sounding association, the expensive but fake letterhead, the phone number that was not real. Dad said he thought the joker was this old guy he used to work with, former shop steward for High Society Hats, one of the companies he'd closed down.

"But I am kind, aren't I?" Dad asked us. "And I'm known for my cakes."

When Dad said he'd drive us to Los Angeles and we could fly from there and it'd be cheaper than flying from St. Louis, we three groaned. Dad was a natural passenger who drove with his head turned sideways or nearly backward, and as children we'd either cowered in fear of the impending crash or hidden from those who passed with their middle fingers raised. I said I could drive, but to my surprise the other three said the same of me, reminded me I used to say I drove fast to get where I was going before my car broke down. We settled on a bus, forty-nine hours to LA, then a flight to Molokai. We could sleep on the bus and take our own food.

"You have the time, right?" Kirk said to me, then smirked.

"Nothing but," I said. "I am rich in time."

Kirk and Ken were rich in wives and children and teaching jobs.

Ken stood up from the table, then laughed and pointed at Dad. "This old guy," he said, "acts like he believes the award exists. Like he wants it."

Dad laughed. "This old guy?" He pointed at himself. "Really?"

Twelve days later, Ken dropped us off at 10 for our 11 p.m. departure, said he could hardly wait to see the gold medal, to bite into the chocolate.

I carried a canvas bag of chips, bananas, bite-sized Snickers, and trail mix onto the bus, as well as an insulated bag of waters and two

1.5-liter bottles of cheap pinot grigio. Dad brought two butter cakes, one for us and one for the lepers. We dropped our provisions on seats A and B, Row 10, right side, then Dad and I took Seats A and B, Row 11. The light-and-dark-blue leatherette seats were wide and almost comfortable with ample legroom, but both armrests were sticky. The three other passengers were men in their late twenties, early thirties, who seemed ill at ease in trying to look comfortable, stretching their jean-covered legs out and emitting small, almost-silent sighs, crossing and then uncrossing their arms, thumbing through sports magazines.

"It has to be my butter cakes," Dad said as the bus merged onto Interstate 44 and gained speed. "The ones for death row."

"You do know there's no award, right?" I said, and I decided I'd give him an award when we got there, make a funny ceremony out of it, a T-shirt with a rainbow across it, a mug that said aloha. I'd take a picture of him holding up whatever it was, and I'd send it to Ken and Kirk. I'd title it "The Hatchet Man Makes Good," though I knew that was too harsh.

Throughout my childhood, Dad served as production manager for a metal-parts company that eventually moved to China. He was the one who closed down both factories, put 115 people out of work, and that put him in demand briefly as a closer. He was eventually hired to do the same for a half-dozen businesses. Ken and Kirk said he walked around his house and theirs, too, during those years, muttering, "Those sons-a-bitches, those godforsaken, hell-spawn, greedy bastards." I was in Houston then, visiting every few months to cheer him up, and I watched the sadness drop deeper over his head with each visit. First, it was with forehead lines, then droopy lids, then bags, then loose skin on his cheeks. Sure, all that was aging, but it was harsher and faster than normal. Ken and Kirk and I told him what he'd told us always: Don't waste time being sad.

Once his skills at closing were no longer needed, he opened a catering business, what we three called an odd choice for one who preferred canned and fried foods, but he claimed he'd been to enough receptions to know the food didn't have to taste good, just look good. He ended up doing retirements, graduations, and funerals, seldom had repeat business, and closed fast, but not before he was awarded the contract to provide last meals for the Missouri condemned. What he called butter cakes were pound cakes made with the whole pound of butter that gave them their name. It was Carol's recipe. He included

one with every last meal, even if not requested. And over the years he'd entered them in baking contests, invariably coming in second, being beaten by flashy desserts with whipped creams and sprinkles and ribbons of icing.

The bus stopped at a McDonald's just west of Oklahoma City a little after eight o'clock the next morning. We ordered only coffee, having stayed up until nearly three, nibbling chips and candy, drinking one whole bottle of wine, telling the same old, funny stories, like the one about Dad's cousin who tied fishing line to dead Great Aunt Clarabelle's hand so she gave a last wave before the coffin lid was closed. "See you soon," the cousin said in falsetto as he made Clarabelle wave. I laughed as I always had. "Course, he was beaten thoroughly after," Dad said. "Those old ones could tear you up good."

As we walked the parking lot perimeter three times, Dad said it was as if hot knives were being jabbed into his knees and ankles with each step, and he wished he had a walking stick. He was seventy-nine, and I'd been expecting the talk of age and need. I was prepared to move in with him if he wanted me to. Or maybe he just wanted to move into a place with other old guys he could sit around and tell stories to all day. It was how he spent much of his time now at the Donut Sack in a strip mall a few blocks from his little yellow house, telling the same stories to the same men, all of them sipping from bottomless cups of dark roast. He said the guys asked for certain stories by name, the one about the postman, for example.

The talk of his encroaching old age didn't come, but I knew when it did it would be funny, Ken's "this old guy" remark a start.

When I was in high school, I excelled at funny stories. I worked part time in a department store, and my sort-of friend, the extra-fat Emily, worked there, too. Emily worked her station by sitting on a stool surrounded by counters of chocolates and sugar and rotating warm nuts. One evening, a leg on her wooden stool snapped in two, and Emily went down hard. When she recovered her breath, she laughed. "This isn't because I eat these nuts," she said as she tried to stand up. I took off early that day and drove her home, thinking her brave to joke about her pain. Her smock and even her skin smelled of warm sugar, and as I took one side and the security guard took another, Emily's arm behind my neck like a thick body pillow, we all laughed at that, too. Turned out, though, Emily had cracked her hip and needed a new one.

Her size worked against her, and two days later she died in surgery. I told Dad only the first part of the story, and he believed Emily to be a strong and funny woman. He said he admired her spirit, and I elaborated on the good parts, making what Emily said while still on the floor even funnier, stuff like, "It was one cashew too many."

As we walked the parking lot in Oklahoma City, Dad wondered out loud. "How would they hear about the cakes all the way in Molokai?" He shrugged. "Course, it's a small world. And stranger things have happened." He smiled at me, his blue eyes seeming bluer, lined, as they were, in red. "Not that there is an award.

"Cheeseburgers with fries and a shake. The most requested meal. Imagine that. There was one Lobster Thermidor. That one a challenge." He was talking about the last-meal requests. I'd heard most of it many times.

"Yeah. One guy wanted only M&M's and a Coke, right?"

"One just had holy communion."

When Dad was closing factories, I called him once a week from Houston with funny stories. I told him about Veronica who'd written a novel, *A Garden of Weeds*, about child abuse being bad. That was the point, I told Dad. It is bad to abuse children. He laughed. Veronica published her book herself, telling me no publisher wanted it because it told the truth. Veronica had a small head on a long neck made longer by intricate dangling earrings that made her move her head slowly as if the circles and chains and beads caused a drag. She went to open mics in grocery stores and bars to read from her book. Once, she made two women in the audience cry. "What's her point?" Dad asked. "Does she think it's wrong to abuse children?" We both laughed. What I didn't say was Trevor, the man I'd moved to Houston with, had left me for Veronica. I also didn't say the State of Texas had taken Veronica's sons from her years earlier.

All three of the other riders got off at Oklahoma City, and when Dad and I got back on the bus, we swapped seats so I had the window. Once we started moving, Dad told the story about the CEO of his old metal-parts company, Lloyd something-or-other. Dad called him Lloyd the Void. He was named "St. Louis Businessman of the Year" just nine months before he closed shop and moved production to China. I'd heard the story often. The speech Lloyd the Void gave at the awards banquet stressed the value of the American worker, said the money and recognition that came with being "St. Louis Businessman of the Year"

143

should be shared by the whole team. "I wrote that part," Dad said. "Yet, when I heard it, I almost fell for it. For a nanosecond, I thought maybe Lloyd wasn't a complete void after all, even if he did speak like he had a wad of cotton stuffed up his nose. Guess I was a good writer. Best part, though, was there were these raw oysters on ice, and they were passed around only at the head table. They were off, so Lloyd and his clones voided all night."

"Roger got me bigger boobs for my birthday." I still had to find a way to make that funny, but I laughed anyway. "Bigger targets for gravity, I guess. I mean, I'm forty-two. Natural, tear-drop-shaped sags."

"Yeah, you said. Boobs from a boob. Think I'll have to give a speech in Molokai?"

"Good one," I said.

He moved to the story of his Uncle Ishmael, the alcoholic postman who began his route as he was meant to each morning. Mere blocks from the start, though, was McGuire's tavern. Ishmael would stop in McGuire's, have what he told the bartender was just one beer for breakfast. A little extra protein. One beer became many, and Ishmael rarely made it past McGuire's, so folks on his route got used to sending their kids to the tavern to sort through the mailbag hanging on the back of his chair. McGuire's liked it cause the kids were often told to bring a bucket of beer back with them. "Amazing," Dad said. "Ish managed to retire from the post office."

I'd seen my Great-Uncle Ish only once, at a family event a few years before he died. His skin was a dull yellow. He appeared to be wrapped in a pee-stained bedsheet.

At two-thirty in the morning, our bus stopped in Albuquerque and a new driver took over. I'd not much noticed our old driver, a large, quiet man with a dark beard, but the new one was hard to ignore. She wasn't quite five feet tall, with black hair thick and coarse as a horse's mane cascading over her shoulders and hiding the embroidered silhouette of a running dog above what should have been her name stitched in white on a blue uniform shirt. Her shirt was missing its sleeves, giving me a nice look at the tattoos covering both arms. Deep red roses in full bloom covered each of her biceps, and their thorny stems wound down and around her arms to her wrists. Though it was early morning, and the bus was lit only by the terminal's floodlights shining in, I saw the roses clearly because she walked back to us, leaned over Row 10 where

our snacks were, and asked if she could have some chips. She'd not eaten all day.

I'd barely nodded before she reached into a bag of ranch tortilla chips and put a large handful in her mouth. She took another, then wiped her hands on her jeans, pulled her hair back so the name Becky was clear above her breast pocket, and said, "Hi. I'm your new driver."

Dad was awake by then, and he shook her hand, said, "Ralph."

"My name's not Becky," she said. "I borrowed this shirt."

Dad reached over the seat into the bag with his butter cakes, broke off a hunk as big as his fist, and handed it to her.

"Thanks," she said. "I'm a prisoner of love. I've been enslaved."

Dad rolled his eyes at me, but I knew the trip had become more exciting for him.

"You get it, right?" Not-Becky said.

"A psychiatrist I saw just one time told me a story," I said. "His mother had a parrot, a blue something-or-other, and the parrot said 'I love you' whenever she entered a room. His mother was the one who taught the parrot to say that, yet she still blushed and smiled when the bird said 'I love you.' As if she believed the bird loved her. As if she had convinced herself the bird's love was something to be desired. Now this psychiatrist, Duckworth, said the bird didn't know what the words meant. If it even understood them as communication, it probably meant to say 'I'm hungry' or 'I hate you.'"

"What did he know about birds?" Not-Becky said. "Was he a veterinarian?" She snorted. "Someone says love, it means love. Take it as it is."

"Gracie," Dad said. "Hope you didn't pay that idiot much."

That was a new funny story.

Dad hadn't known I'd seen a psychiatrist, nor had he known of my weightlessness, not even way back when I moved to Houston with Trevor so we could both write for the oil companies. I was like a helium balloon lost in the sky then, drifting toward doom. Dad would remember I'd said Trevor was my love, but I'd not ever said I was Trevor's. I'd never told him Trevor's complaint at the end, either, that I was too often facetious. Roger and Scott, Roger's predecessor, both had echoed Trevor at times, Roger quoting some study that people who knew how to laugh usually also knew how to cry, but I didn't seem to. Did he want me to cry, I asked, and he said of course not.

Dad knew about my work for Shell Oil's energy-assistance program, our joke then the truth that real assistance would be lowering prices,

but I'd not told him of the meanness I found in myself while working for Shell. Once, I moved a couple down the list because they seemed like liars, though there was no evidence of that. Their finances checked out. Later, I realized it was that they had that squinty-eyed look of Trevor's parents, and I already knew he'd fallen for Veronica. Some time later, a young man who smelled like unwashed socks wouldn't look at me directly, shrugged in answer to most questions, and when he said he needed air-conditioning to sleep, I said just pass out on the barstool you so clearly spend most of your life on.

Not-Becky joined us for lunch at the McDonald's in Gallup, New Mexico. At first, we were all quiet, biting into our burgers, dragging fries through ketchup, staring into space, but Not-Becky stopped eating, put her burger down and took a breath, hesitated for half a second. "Just the three of us," she finally said. "We can go wherever we want." She smiled. "Where do you want to go?" When we didn't answer right away, she said she'd go to Yuma.

"Los Angeles for us," Dad said. I noticed he had ketchup on his T-shirt sleeve.

Not-Becky smiled so big I could see most of her teeth. "So what's in LA?"

"Molokai," I said. "We're going to Molokai, Not-Becky. Dad's getting an award. For kindness." I laughed, nudged his elbow with mine.

"For my butter cakes."

Not-Becky smiled big again. "I love that, you calling me Not-Becky. I told you I was a victim of love, right? I want to take a small detour to see him." She told us her name was Sue and her love was for a man she met last summer in Chicago, a migrant worker from Mexico with crooked teeth and rounded shoulders. His name was Pete, not Pedro. Who wouldn't expect his name to be Pedro? But no, it was Pete, so she called him Not-Pedro. It was their joke and the reason she found our calling her Not-Becky funny. He was picking lettuce in Yuma now, better money than Illinois and a short hop across the border.

Dad said he had come in second place eleven times, eleven different contests. His butter cakes had. "National contests," he added.

Sue said she'd asked for this route so she could stop and see Not-Pedro. That was, if the passengers were willing to be put out just a bit for love. She proposed that when we got to Buckeye, Arizona, we'd head south for a short time, then go to Yuma, then, after some fast

smoochie-smoochie, we'd race to LA. We were scheduled to get to LA close to midnight and were booked into an airport hotel. If we did things Sue's way, we'd get into LA at five in the morning, six at the latest. Our flight left at two p.m., so we'd have lots of time but would've saved the hotel expense. "One more night on the bus," she said, "and you can save enough for one big luau."

"I'm in," Dad said, as I knew he would. "Ever been in jail?"

Sue said no but looked happy he'd considered it possible.

"More than a few years ago," Dad said, settling back into his plastic chair for one of his favorite stories, "a man being put to death by the state of Missouri said he wanted chicken-fried steak for his last meal. Know what that is? Hard-fried, gristly cubed steak smothered with cream gravy, usually mashed potatoes, and limp green beans. Anyway, the steak was cooked too hard. The guy going to die couldn't cut into the steak, not with the knives they allowed him, anyway. Way I heard it, the guard tried to help, too, used his pocketknife. The nearly dead man took the steak up in his hands and tried to bite into it but no luck there either. He ate the mashed potatoes and beans but threw the steak on the concrete floor, said someone could maybe use it as a boot scraper. His last words were: "That was the worst meal I've ever had. In my whole life. Bar none." I was catering a few events for the prisons then, so I heard about it. I applied for and got the last-meal account."

"At least he doesn't need repeat business," I said, and Not-Becky laughed with me.

"Those about to die should have something sweet. Butter cake. And jokes. I told one of the wardens that as long as they get last meals, they should get last jokes too. Who wouldn't want to go laughing? Not likely, though. They don't even get alcohol with their last meals, as if there's something unsavory about dying while drunk."

Sue snorted.

"I work hard on the meals, learning how to make whatever they want. Crab Rangoon once. And I always throw in the butter cakes, requested or not."

Sue asked if they ever had been requested, and Dad admitted they had not. Still, he knew they were appreciated. And now the award. "I'm known for those butter cakes," he said.

"I didn't hate the bite I had," Sue said.

"The lepers don't seem to have a second place," he said. "Just the gold medal."

147

I wrapped up my half-eaten cheeseburger, held it out toward Dad on the palm of my hand, and said, "Ralph Newstead, I hereby present you with this first-place award for your butter cakes, the symbol of your amazing kindness." Dad blushed and, missing only a beat, chuckled.

Eight years earlier, I took a bottle of over-the-counter sleeping pills and washed it down with as much Scotch as I could swallow without hearing it slosh about in my gut. I couldn't say why. I got in my bed, closed my eyes, and imagined not waking up. But I did wake up, all cotton-mouth and dizzy. That morning, I found Doctor Duckworth through an online search. His photo made him look like the Groucho Marx character his name implied, so I made an appointment. He said I hadn't wanted to die, just wanted attention. How could that be, I asked him. No one knew of the attempt. I was alone. He shrugged. Now that Trevor was gone, I asked, should I stay or move back to St. Louis? In response, he told me the mother-and-parrot story then said it didn't matter what I decided to do. He said I should stop caring so much. His thick, black moustache did not seem to move with his lips. He said depressed people don't care what happens, and happy people don't, either, and his point was depression and happiness can be exactly the same.

When Sue left the bus at eight that evening, she said Not-Pedro worked, like all the lettuce pickers, until every speck of light was gone. His visitor work permit required him to go back across the border each night, but this one night he'd hide out on this side. "Why lepers?" she asked before she left. "Why would lepers be giving out an award?"

"Lepers like kindness, too," Dad said. "Why not lepers?"

Dad awoke around seven, the sun already well above the Walmart and the entire sky a white glare. He checked his watch and scanned the horizon. We were supposed to be at the airport between noon and one, and the airport was five hours away in good traffic. "We're not late yet," he said. "Let's not panic." He wanted to believe Sue was too smart to get arrested in some sort of immigration sting and most likely was unable to drag herself away from Not-Pedro. But at eight-twenty, even though he hated to rat anyone out, he called Greyhound's 800 number. We did have an awards ceremony to get to, after all. "A gold medal," he said. "This may be my only gold medal." We managed to get through the automated responses and then took turns telling our story to the various representatives we were transferred to, five in all, one who laughed out loud. Eventually, we were taken to the Yuma station, all hope of getting

to LA on time gone. We were told Greyhound didn't have a driver named Sue or any variation of Sue on its many routes. The good news was a bus would be going to LA in just a few hours, and all parts of our trip were free.

I sent a text to Ken and to Kirk: We were trapped on a bus in Yuma, and Dad thinks there's an award. But in a Yuma donut shop, Sweet Somethings, we sat on swivel stools and split the last bear claw, and Dad said there was no reason to go to Molokai. I nodded, relieved. "We've always known the award was just an excuse for fun," I said.

"No, I mean because we'll be too late. The ceremony's tonight," he said. "We'll miss it."

He swiveled his stool so he faced me. He looked at me with a clear, firm gaze, not seeming confused at all, no half-smile about to break out, either.

"We can call and check," I said. "Once we're on the island." Call the not-real number of the fake association. "Maybe there'll be someone to talk to."

He nodded. "Gold-plated is OK, too. It doesn't have to be solid gold."

He came to my hotel room that evening for help with his speech. Dress rehearsal, he called it, so he wore his wedding tuxedo I hadn't known he'd packed, the jacket too tight to button and smelling of moth balls. He paced from the door to the window as he reworked and practiced his remarks. He thanked the Missouri condemned and the entire Missouri Prison system. He thanked Carol for the recipe. He told the Uncle Ish story as an example of kindness. "Is it too long?" he asked a few times, and though I said always yes, he continued to add to it, finally including my addict mother and Not-Becky, who maybe was not Sue either, as examples of something I could no longer keep track of.

When the Hawaiian Air flight attendant said aloha and mahalo and showed us the oxygen, I turned to Dad, ready to say, "Please accept this safety brochure in honor of your lifetime achievement," but our jet rattled and bucked its way down the runway, then pointed its nose up, and Dad reached for and held my hand, squeezing hard. This was always our favorite part, being torn from the Earth and pushed into the sky as gravity was defeated briefly but surely. I closed my eyes then and saw a noseless man in a bright shirt dance across cliffs like folds of green velvet. In one hand, he carried a necklace of flowers pinker than Dad's skin. In the other, a gold medal, catching the sun.

# SOCIAL MEDIA PETERSEN
## LIZZY PLATFORM

Somewhere a woman from my past posts each new waistband
of her pregnancy. Persist: to go beyond the threshold
of necessity. Her waist, divided infinitely into points. Measure her

expansiveness and tell the time through her growth, waiting
for the womb to drop like a comet through a black hole.
One day pregnant, the next round. An infant crooked in her arm.

Infant: to be speechless. Infinity: to be boundless.
Aristotle asserts neither is true, just a chattered will to divide.
A matter of less less. And to continue to.

Each click of the image changes her—something else grows. Divides
between my realm and hers and her stepfather's and a coworker's.
With each click, a new "us" dissects her. And conflates her

with every other pregnancy, a never-ending pregnancy
until I am numb to the slow explosion, fathoming less and less:
a tape measure snapped back into its shell.

# LIFE KOERTGE
## RON ON THE FARM

It's not easy: weather, predators,
creditors. I'm just glad I've got Minnie.

She'll unruffle a skittish mare nine times
out of ten. She'll play with the yearlings.

She'll sleep with a foal and the mama will
let her. Minnie's just a hell of a goat.

And a coyote's never going to get her.
She's got the blood to survive. Her daddy

was the Judas goat at National Beef.
Had the horns, that funny little beard,

had the little bell. He'd usher a hundred sheep
toward the killing floor, then turn away at just

the right time so he could do it again after
lunch. Minnie's not like that. She'll get

a horse to water and make him drink, too.
Except, I have this dream where she's leading

it all away, everything I own traipsing along
behind her. Or the nightmare that almost stops

my heart where I go out to the barn and there's
Minnie with thirty pieces of silver.

# TIGERS PACE AZA AT 1 A.M.

Not where I expected lilies,
in a round vase beside the dumpster,
with their wide pink grins
and the sticky, obscene stigma
tonguing out at the center.

Not the time for them, either: just past one,
my skin still humid from fog machine.
They cock their extravagant heads
at the city-dimmed night sky,
petals striping muscular over sepals.

Their sweet smell, almost an ache,
burns orange as anthers
in the corners of my eyes.
I look around for their tamers,
up and down the street.

# NOT EVEN LOONEY
## GEORGE A DECENT WIND TO BLAME

A gnome-on-speed of a man, a professor,
on an Irish TV talk show, talks,
with avid seriousness & passion,
about the mistake of building estates
that block fairy paths. Doors locked,
even chained at night, mornings are

found open, not even a decent wind
to blame. Progress shouldn't be
totally amnesiac, his point,
& fairy paths & fairy glens should be
sacred. What he wants is
a respect for the past, for the lore

that got us through. The young, he says,
need to listen to the stories. They need
to believe. "Foockin' fairies,"
a Cork teen says. "Foock, what a foockin'
crock tey is." The fairies have it
right, refusing to believe in *this* world.

# ACADIANA LEMEROND
## SAUL ORANGE GROVES

He wasn't even close to being the journalist he thought he was. Not that good in bed, either. The last time we were together I had one of those bone-shivering orgasms that for a few moments made me forget he was dying and that I'd divorced him, just like I'd hoped it would. After I rolled next to him and put my arm across his chest, he said, "That was really good for me," then I remembered. If there was ever a time when he cared about my success over his, he never said it.

Two weeks later, I'm hosting his wake while I'm on the verge of getting fired, and there's a chance the world as we know it will be changed forever.

Out of the window I can see a large silver sphere next to the blooming white magnolia trees, which means the aliens have landed. Steve was a damn good journalist. As sources, the aliens were exclusive to Steve. There are also fifty other mourning journalists outside, and I'm inside stirring my stew. The pot holds ten gallons.

It's good the aliens have come. They are more famous and more loved than the president. I tell Diana my memories of Steve are like the white beans I put in hours ago. I say, "I can remember them being beautifully delicious and whole, but now all that's left is the thick, salty taste of something that probably never should have been there in the first place."

Diana takes her hands away from her face and wipes them on her tan apron with white printed tulips on it. "Why do you keep comparing him to stew?" she asks.

She's looking up at the slow rotating ceiling fan with tears in her eyes. I want to tell her that it's not like her dog died, even if they were cousins. She knows he was a cheat.

"He was such a good man," says Diana. "And thirty-five is so young. Do you think he got cancer from all those video games?"

Coulda been. Or he coulda got cancer because everybody in his family gets cancer. Also, Steve didn't exactly live clean. He smoked and drank. He spent a lot of time in the sun. He liked eating red meat. He'd say he was going to play basketball with his buddies then stay out late, sleep around, and never use protection. He liked to stand in front of the microwave. He was a mother-fucker. A big, cheating mother-fucker, and I've always felt cancer likes that sort of person.

I smell burnt brisket and realize I should have taken it out of the oven forty-five minutes ago.

Yesterday, my boss told me that he was both sad and sorry my ex died, but if I didn't start breaking real stories, I was going to have to start looking for another job. It's good the aliens are here. Steve was their insider, and he's dead. I'm his ex-wife and a much better journalist, so it's reasonable I could take Steve's place. It would be an honor to his memory. The best thing he's ever done for me, really.

"His breath," I say to Diana, "smelled like burnt beef brisket when it didn't smell like Pabst beer and Kool cigarettes." It's a wonder any one person would want to have sex with him, let alone so many.

"Brisket? Really?" She's stopped crying but still watches the fan.

I put the smoldering brisket by the window. The silver sphere that is twice the size of the pole barn it has landed next to is filled with five aliens who are more famous than the A-list of the A-list, and who have said to Steve, off the record, that they want to make Earth more orange. On the left side of the sphere are my white magnolia trees, which is next to the gathering of journalists who are all here to mourn my husband. Half of these people are ladies. Half of those ladies, I'm pretty sure, have been with Steve.

I walk over to the fridge, get out the salad, look at the pickled beets on top, and say, "He's like pickled beets you shouldn't use because they've been canned and in the pantry for six years and …."

"Mary Ann," she stops me. "If you compare Steve to that salad, I will not help you serve those people who are waiting outside for you to feed them."

I look over to the brisket.

"No," she says. "Not the brisket either."

Outside, there's more than a dozen picnic tables. Fifty people is a lot of people even when they aren't journalists. The silver sphere has

opened, and a ramp now leads from the opening to the ground. The gray aliens wear white robes and are as tall as basketball hoops and thin as cancer patients.

I remember when they first moved into Mars. I had just started high school, and they made me think anything was possible, like I could move to another solar system someday. Get away from Louisiana. Get away from Lafayette. Steve was the first to interview them. He was the reason I studied journalism. The reason I interned for Steve and then married Steve.

Now the aliens are here, and they need representation and every journalist here at this wake knows it and like me hope they can make some kind of inroads with these Martians.

I take two large platters out from the pantry. I tell Diana to take out the pudding.

The five aliens sit down next to one of the picnic tables they are too tall to sit in and ask, all at once, when the gumbo is coming.

"There isn't any gumbo" says a woman in a pillbox funeral veil who I think I sort of know and am pretty sure Steve has fucked. The body in the form-fitting black cocktail dress is certainly something that would be his type. "We're having stew and brisket." She reaches into her purse to pull out a pen and notepad.

"Oh," say the aliens, saying nothing about making the Earth more orange. Their faces are expressionless, and so it's hard to tell if they are disappointed about the absence of gumbo.

"I was wondering if there was anything you could tell me about the rumors that …," starts the women in the cocktail dress.

"Trust me when I say you'll love my stew," I interrupt because I will not allow this woman to have both my husband and my story. I place one of the vegetable trays on the table before them. "Try the pickled beet salad," I say to women who probably fucked my husband. "Steve and I canned them the summer before we got married."

"I loved your husband; he was always so engaging," say the aliens all at once. They have big, oval eyes with lanky arms and large hands, each with six fingers, each the length of marching-band batons.

They say, "When I first met him, it was in a green room at *Good Morning Big Country*. Or was it *Headline News*?" The aliens pause for a moment, trying to remember, before saying, "It doesn't matter. He had such a way with words."

I ask if I can talk to them in the kitchen. I tell them there's stew in there and do it because I need them to be my source for all news that is Martian. I need them because everyone on this planet who matters loves them.

"Is this about the orange thing?" ask the five aliens.

I say that yes, it is, and walk the aliens back toward the house, telling them they're probably not going to be able to fit in the kitchen but they could probably just stick their heads in. They tell me it's no problem. They say if I move the table they'll be all be able to crawl in and lie on the floor flat, facing toward the ceiling, which is what they end up doing.

They lie on my kitchen floor and stare at my ceiling fan. "I love the amber of your eyes," they say.

I have no idea what they are talking about. I ask them if they would like something to eat. They say they do not.

"The new Earth is exactly like the old one," they say. "It has everything you know and love, except, you know, it's more orange."

I write this down on my notepad.

"More orange?" I ask.

One of the aliens turns their head to the right, and I look over to the open window and see the woman with the pillbox veil peering in over the still-smoldering brisket along with another woman who I think is the anchor for the local public radio station. I imagine that if their eyes were olives that they'd make a nice garnish for the brisket sandwiches.

"Could you excuse us, please?" I ask. "We're grieving."

"Oh," says Ms. Public Broadcasting. "We didn't mean to interrupt. It's just that we could smell the brisket and, well, it smells delicious, and we were wondering when it was going to come out?"

"Soon," I reply.

"It's just, there's so many hungry people out here," she says.

"I know," I say.

"And the stew?" she asks.

"Also soon," I say, then momentarily pause before adding, "just not as soon as the brisket." I then sweep my hand through the air in a shooing motion, hoping to shoo the greedy, cheating harlots away from my open window, and they do, they shoo.

I turn back to the aliens. "More orange?" I ask again.

"Yes," says the gray alien. "The Earth wasn't pastel enough. We live on Mars and have a telescopic window, and the earth clashed with the sun on most days. But vaporizing the old Earth was not a big deal. The new Earth has everything the old one does."

I quickly write this down, then stop and look at what I've written because something about it looks off to me. "Did you just say you were going to vaporize the Earth?" I ask.

I hear a crash and look toward the open back door. Diana is standing there. She's dropped an empty food tray. One of my Waterford serving trays is shattered at her feet.

"Vaporize?" she says while staring blankly at what is ostensibly nothing.

"You don't need to worry," says the aliens, who then all reach their right arms into the air and snap their fingers. I look over to Diana, and she's holding a tray that is no longer shattered but whole and unbroken. "The new Earth has you. It has mountains. It has all the same TV shows and movies and animals and wars. It's just more orange. The seas are more orange. The snow is more orange. The grasses and plants, too."

I write all of this down and say nothing until I've finished with the list that includes all the things they've mentioned: TV, movies, mountains, animals, and wars. I want to break this story. Vaporizing the Earth, though, does not sound good to me.

"And all of the people?" I ask.

"Yes," they say. "All of the same people do all of the same things," the aliens pause and then wave their hands in the air, adding, "just more orange."

I do not like the sound of any of this and am just about to say that it sounds great when Diana screams, "You can't do that!" And then everyone is looking at her. "We don't want that. You'll kill us all!" she adds, and I'm happy she's said it.

They look to me. "You think there are Earthlings who might be concerned about being more orange?" they ask.

"Sure," I say. "I'm not sure everyone's going to agree on the color, but I think the vaporization," I pause, trying to think of the right words, "I think that would be the biggest concern."

"Really?" asks the aliens.

Diana walks into the kitchen and stands hip to hip with me with her mouth hanging open. She takes in a deep breath and puts her hands on her carrot-colored apron with marigolds printed on it.

"Really," I say.

"Well," say the aliens. "I mean, we already did it."

Diana grabs my arm and holds it tight like we've just gone through a near-death experience together, but I don't understand. So I say, "I don't understand."

"There's not much to understand," says the aliens, still staring up at the ceiling fan, tugging at the folds of their orange robes. "We vaporized the old Earth. The new Earth is more orange."

I look around. So does Diana.

"Nothing looks more orange," says Diana.

"Of course not," says the aliens. "Because it's the same. This Earth has always been more orange. The old Earth is vaporized. It's gone. You've never seen it. How would you be able to tell?"

"Tell that the Earth is more orange?" I repeat.

"This Earth," corrects the aliens. "This Earth is more orange than the last one. You've never seen the last one, so how would you be able to tell?"

"Tell that this new Earth is more orange?" I say again.

"Yes," say the aliens.

Diana leans in and speaks softly into my ear, "I think they're saying that they vaporized the Earth, which we were on, and then they created a new Earth, and that you and me are new us's, and that we can't tell because the new us never saw the old, less-orange Earth and less-orange us's." She then turns to the aliens. "Is that correct?" she asks.

"Yes," say the aliens, who are still staring up at the ceiling fan.

Diana makes eye contact with me, raising her eyebrows and twirling her eyes around her sockets as if to say that these aliens are crazy. Really crazy. More eccentric than anyone had even thought. I give a slight nod so she knows I agree.

"But I still want you to be my publicist," says the aliens.

"You mean journalist-insider," I correct. I try to remember if the carrots in my stew were more orange than they were supposed to be.

"Whatever," they say. "Steve always did such a wonderful job, and he always spoke so very highly of you. I'd love it if you did for me what he did."

The idea that Steve has said one good thing about me since we'd taken our wedding vows is not something I readily accept.

"Steve mentioned me?" I ask. Steve mentioned me. The old me. But they still want to work with the new me. I rub my hands together and decide I don't feel any different and that I must still be me.

159

"Of course," say the aliens. "He was constantly going on about you. Mary Ann-this, he would say, and Mary Ann-that. We were actually very excited to meet you today."

I don't know what to say and stand in the middle of my kitchen looking down at the unreadable faces of these aliens, and I don't keep track for how long. I saw Steve for the last time, lying in his casket, at the funeral this morning. Was his skin more orange than it was supposed to be?

Diana looks at me and squeezes my arm again. "See?" she says. "I told you he was a good guy."

The aliens wiggle out of my kitchen and then stand up again once they're outside.

"We'll be back to talk with you soon."

"I'm going to go," they say. And they begin walking away toward their sphere. They look back, and we can see several people moving away from the picnic tables toward us. All my guests want what I have, and they don't know they can't have it, that all they're getting is burnt brisket and undercooked stew.

Several of the journalists try to ask the aliens questions as they walk.

How is your visit? they ask. The aliens do not answer.

The sun is bright, but I can't tell if it's more orange than it's supposed to be.

Do you still like the system the same as when you first moved in? they ask. The aliens do not answer.

They walk in their orange robes past the orange magnolia trees, get into their sphere, and take off.

Everyone watches it disappear toward a sun that makes the clouds look like marigolds.

I tell Diana to go back inside and get the stew ready and that I'll be in to help her in a couple of minutes. It's nice that I get to stay employed, which is the job that used to be Steve's, and that he actually said good things about me now and again, but I'm happy this is his wake. Given enough time, I'm sure I'll be able to forgive him. Mostly because, with enough time, I feel like I'll forget why I ever hated him in the first place. I pull a petal off my orange magnolia tree on the way back inside.

# THE OTHER SIDE TEAL
## JASON OF THE MIRROR OF LIES

Marjorie spit seedy nightmares from the face of the black mirror, so if I lied she probably heard it. Then some rain. I kicked myself. Said I forgot. I said the dog died of cancer. The summer house foreclosed. I quit my job at the fracking firm as soon as brunch.

"I won't tell you everything," I said, biting my nails, but I was talking to a ghost. Her time was precious. She was missing for months. At the wake, we mourned properly.

The mirror was a gift. Arrived unpolished with no sender, so I scoured the empty face, twice, checking for ruptures. In the heated garage, clear-seeing and supranormal, I slit the film wrap with rusty scissors, waxed the cold black of my doom with a work rag. Something inside me balked at Marjorie's divine visit, pimply and exposed.

Later, I blotted my eyes with the candied patchwork of an injured towel. Colleagues were up and had gone to church, but for me it was so early and bright.

I didn't have the fear of God, though when Marjorie was hard up she almost loved me. I didn't believe her, not for her trying. Another, darker thought: She owed me nothing.

My hands searched her face for answers, secret lives. An old letter from Marjorie read I was better off alone. I was not allowed or even supposed to mention that. Best I didn't think of her at all.

Marjorie had no sister; I was a convert. An itch. I rowed with the disembodied voices overhead. The fact was, Marjorie never called. She never said someone I used to love tried to throw me off the bridge.

There was Marjorie talking and then a snort. A loogie, and I caught everything. It was more than one—she was coughing streams of it into a napkin in the other world.

My steps upstairs were labored, clownish. I let the mirror collect dust until it didn't.

CLARK

CLAYTON ADAM **OUROBORIC**

From the mist of insects flying above me, pairs fall
like ash or skin. The small one on my forearm climbs

the backside of the other, which bucks and turns
a circle, snapping after its rear, but he's already in

and clamped to her abdomen. When we fought

yesterday I was wrong and I wasn't and I must
show my wife I'm sorry because the transmutation

between *me* and *me and mine* is material. This family
I met at work donated the father's body but asked

to keep his back skin and the serpentine crest

tattooed across it. Like bickering again about who does
or doesn't do enough housework, repurposing a father's

epidermis as a lampshade heirloom is absurd and not.
The bloodless outer layer of the skin is only one

millimeter thick, so as the female chases him

and thus herself once more, they feel my pulse below.
He tries to exit her but can't—they have to work

together now, clambering apart until they're separate.
But when she charges at him, he's too fast to flight,

leaving her on my arm. Alone, I can follow the blood,

trailing a vessel back to its aorta, but I've yet to capture
with my body all I mean. My wife once asked me,

*Why is it we always love the sad song?* We came
home from dinner, and I made us drinks. She turned

on an album and lay down on the kitchen hardwood.

I joined her there, feeling nothing beneath my soles,
and when the song came on, she set it for repeat.

163

# SATELLITE WEATHER

WALTER BARGEN

Behind the smile and fast-moving
time-lapsed satellite pictures on the screen,
where clouds cover and uncover
a continent of colors in the blink

of an eye, before the exhaust and dust
of a city pinpoints and settles over the tangle
of two rivers, before a high plains is called great,
a distant ocean is fathomed,

or the pistol pulled in the Douglas Park
fires another argument I hear that no records
are being broken, just the same
old tune playing between

the boiling ears of sundown
and dim humid dawn. But around the house
the wind, as if one eyelash
is caught in a hurricane and blinks loose,

lifts the trees and strips their leaves,
leaving the difficult anatomy
of an overheated late autumn.
On the porch every direction

threatens, and with each gust
the leaves crawl toward me,

## SATELLITE WEATHER

an army of castoff gloves
worn out holding to a season's

arbitrary light. Perhaps it's only
a beating blood that has their
thousand brown palms turned up
and shaking, cupping to hear

the chorus of their own scratchy
Victorola voices playing in evenings
spinning dark, a final encore of leaves
before counting tomorrow's cold hearts.

WALTER BARGEN

# MANGER

As a boy no doubt he too had been made to wear
an *azabache*, a discreet jet amulet, to ward off
the evil eye. He did not recall wearing one,
but as an adolescent he noticed all the children
of neighbors and his little cousins donned them on chains,
along with a medal of the Virgin. The girls
would wear them on tiny gold safety pins
on their dress lapels and later move them
to their bra straps. We brandish them, an aunt
would confide, to guard us in our sprung-
trap hour, "Those first years of exile,"
she would sigh. How could an amulet
ward off the tactical evils of the pensive heart
floated on the streets men paved
to overtake their kind?
Streets upon which to head home from work
or course the city of errand and boredom.
Avenues that netted biting hopes as casually
as abundantly, like startled creatures bursting
the rugged if ripe nets. How could a tiny amulet
hold all the blood dark at bay, the lurk of condition,
the dawn machinery that sets smallness going?
No more than a manger could hold
its carnage of straw. No more than a stomach
could stay timeless full with a single fruit of its claws.

# IN WHICH COVEY
## CHARLOTTE I ACTUALLY GET
## WHAT I THOUGHT I WANTED

i would have been bored. endless
monotony, monogamy, missionary. always
a lightness, a kind word. i would have burned
for a kind of darkness, the kind i get
from drinking too much, too quick, the dark that ends
in a stranger's bed with vomit
on sheets. i would have grown
tired of our happiness, our breakfast
dates, our long walks on the beach. i would have slipped
whiskey when we grabbed coffee from
your favorite shop, thought of the barista bending
me over while you paid for my drink.

# THE CABRAL CIRCLE

Before, they were limited to pharmaceutical
instructions and specialized dictionaries.
They were vague, occasional, virtual.
Then they turned to frequent
guests, quite intimate:
arthritis, arterial sclerosis, cirrhosis,
otosclerosis, osteoporosis,
neuromas, fibromas, melanomas.
They were tightening the circle,
migrating from mental abstraction
to the real bodies of people,
flesh bone fingernails and teeth,
people close by, at our very side.
With aching gut
we measure now the gap
between vocabulary word and fact.

*Translated from the Portuguese by Alexis Levitin*

CABRAL
ASTRID **TROCHANTER**

Unexpectedly the word *trochanter*
comes from the dictionary and presents itself to you,
an intruder in your body's flesh and bone.
It crosses through your anaesthetized condition
imposing itself through osteoporosis and bursitis.
And then, in shock, you begin to think of the bundle
of unconscious parts you share.
Your body an infinite ambulatory
continent whose map you have lost,
a long list of liquids and of solids.
And you discover there's another kind of sleep,
in which the body drifts abstracted,
as if without a captain at the helm.

*Translated from the Portuguese by Alexis Levitin*

# SOLITUDE

The stone masonry wall is damp and covered in a musty film of mold. There is a faint, fetid smell. Colored lights rotate continuously, and there are faraway-but-close sounds of car tires, cheap music, and indistinguishable conversation.

They sit side by side on the sofa, his hand in hers. They are skinny and bushy haired, and their drooping eyelids are swollen. They've been sitting here, in hibernation mode, for a very long time, covered by a thick coating of dust. In the crannies of their immobile bodies, spiders have woven webs that no breeze disturbs.

Their chests rise and fall, and the quiet sound of their inhalations alone belie the certainty that they are dead. There is not even the flutter of an eyelid: Their eyes, permanently open, are fixed on the opposite wall.

All the walls are bare except for the one with the liquid crystal display TV flashing ever-changing pictures: a dubbed Turkish series,; nude women cavorting to the tune of some vulgar melody; *The Oprah Winfrey Show*; commercials advertising cooking oil, feminine pads, and a mobile phone; *Who Wants to Be A Millionaire*, a news program whose two relaxed anchors shake their heads in a deliberate show of gravitas; *Star Academy*; and a Hollywood action film being replayed for the nth time with the obligatory car chases, guns, and "fuck" translated as "damn." The colors flicker endlessly, mirrored in their sallow eyes.

Complete obscurity abruptly descends following the crackle of an electric short circuit overhead. Before the screen dies, the flickering colored images are momentarily distorted, and as the last one briefly fixes onto their eyes, total darkness envelops the room.

The silence is brief.

"Hey. Get up and open the window," she says.

"How would I know to do that? I've been sitting on this sofa like you ever since I've known I was sitting on the sofa watching the window. I only know what you know, we've watched it all from this window together. I don't know how to open or close it, and we've never closed the window—it's always been open. Shouldn't I know how to close it in order to know how to open it?"

"Didn't you hear what I said, dammit? Get up and open the window," she says.

"I've learned so many things from the window. I've seen magical worlds and beautiful women, god-humans and machine-humans, massacres and defeats, victories and broken hearts. And sex, oh the sex! Did you see how that girl in the commercial was humping the chocolate bar? Now that's what I call a commercial! But the window didn't teach me how to close or open it. It's always been open. Don't you think that's strange?"

"I'm tired of your excuses, you loser. Don't you understand that we will suffocate and die with the window closed? I'm suffocating right now. Suffocating," she says.

"Well, why don't we try seeing what it's like to have the window closed just this once? That's exactly what I'm thinking right now and, to be more precise, I'm wondering why we didn't try and extend our arms and heads from the window? Why didn't we call out to one of those people sitting outside or passing by? I could've asked one of those women humping on the sofa for a bar of chocolate. I could've joined the protest at 10 Downing Street. I could've invited that singer to sit with us. Some singer she was! The only thing you could hear was the sound of all that silicone! I could've helped the emergency medics with that kid who was riddled with shrapnel holes. What was he screaming? I don't remember anymore. But we remained silent, just watching. I should've poked my head out of the window."

"Ohhhh. I'm suffocating here. You asshole, just open the window. You're jailing me here, killing me ...." She was screaming by now, and her screams grew louder and louder until they disappeared up the big opening in the ceiling, reverberated through the large pipes, and then the smaller ones, smaller, and smaller, and smaller ....

171

☾

The glass almost broke after slipping from between the housewife's soapy fingers as she heard a voice coming up through the sink: "Ohhhh. I'm suffocating here .... Open the window." In his brand-new suit and with a laptop in his briefcase, the twenty-something man recently hired by a large financial company lost his footing and almost tripped over the voice coming up from the sewer, saying, "You asshole. You're jailing me here, killing me ... open the window." And the old man who had popped a Viagra pill and was lathering up with scented soap under the hot shower almost slipped over the voice rising up between his feet: "You're killing me ... open the window."

"Hello, nine-one-one? Yes, hello. There's a voice coming up the sink drain. Yes, yes. Incomprehensible words, something about a closed window ... OK. You're going to take care of it? Thank you very much."

"Hello, nine-one-one? Yes. I was walking in the street and I heard strange voices inside the sewer ... something about suffocation and death and a window .... OK, I knew you'd look into it. Have a good day."

"Hello ... I want to report something that happened earlier today. There were strange voices coming up the drain in the shower. A window, and jail, and things I didn't understand. You say there are other similar reports? It's not just me hearing those things? And you're addressing the problem? Oh, OK! You sure move fast. Bye."

In the midst of the large valley in the city of hills, the bodies of exhausted foreign workers shuddered as they bore down on the pneumatic drills rebounding against the pressure of their arms. Nearby, a large yellow earth-digger drove its huge metal boring-post into the ground, and bulldozers cleared the accumulated debris.

The crater was ten meters deep, and the crew sent out by the authorities used special ropes to scale down to the bottom. From there, they followed the city's massive sewers.

"Drop the hose," one of them said, speaking into a microphone dangling in front of his mouth, as two others examined a tangled mass of wires. An ear-splitting scream came out of the large opening to the side: "Open the window, you loser .... I'm suffocating .... I'm going to die."

Four of the crewmen fixed wooden planks over the opening and crisscrossed them with metal rods. No sooner had the two guys with the wires called out, "Ready now, sir," than the screaming from below stopped. The faraway-but-close sounds of car tires, cheap music, and indistinguishable conversation rushed in, as faint and flickering colored lights filtered through the wooden planks and the metal rods.

"Start pumping," said the dangling microphone guy, and everything was drowned in liquid cement.

*Translated from the Arabic by maia tabet*

# JANIS BENTLEY
## ROY JOPLIN

It's 1970. Dick Cavett asks her how you tear a muscle singing.
She tells him, laughing. Shakes the red-feathered boa in her hair.
She says there's a fire within, shows him what she means, and her
performance is an argument for getting the hell out of Texas. She
is preaching from the Book of Janis in the gospel of rock 'n' roll.
She'd like us to repent for the worst sin of all, our lifelessness.
When the refineries and oil wells of Port Arthur, Texas are gone,
the scrap steel dragged to the rim of some landfill and tossed in—
when the multiple slaughters of the twenty-first Century are finished,

half a million or so egrets of the Gulf covered in tar yet again,
disappeared after having been thrown on the fires of the Modern,
they'll still be trying to make sense of such a blinding intensity.
It's like she wanted to dispel mortality itself as rain in the dark
and send it elsewhere to get reinvested with the spark of Feeling.
This is what it is to live once and know heaven for the lie it is.
This is what it's like to hear the tick of a Geiger counter and gauge
the shared losses and pain on a scale of one to ten for the last time.
How do you pull a muscle in the act of singing? How can you not?

# FROM INCHES AWAY PERCHIK
## SIMON HIS FINGER CAN'T MISS

You lower your voice and dig
till it comes up empty
stays in place though you

are the only one who talks
as the sound dirt makes
when taken away night after night

to fill the hole in this bed
—from such a darkness
you carry up the Earth

to look for the sun
where an afternoon should be
and there you wait

gently pushed along
by some hillside on tiptoe
quietly leaving your mouth.

\*

You lean into this tree as if its roots
struck something made from wood
no longer moves, became an island

with mountains laid out in rows
and though they have no arms
they open them when someone

is left close by—under such a weight
their hands break apart the Earth
from feeling their way around it

grave after grave, blinded by moonlight
as the chunks you never saved
form this nearly empty night

with nothing but the bright green hole
this dying tree drains, keeps dry
between what you wanted and the shine.

\*

From inches away his finger can't miss
—the other kid plays dead, falls arm over arm
the way all games come with a well,

are filled with wishes hardened into stones
sure the Earth would go along
though there's no splash—what you hear

is the thud that purifies each death
as one aimless night followed by another
overflowing and this park

becomes the sudden laughter
you no longer get to be
are waiting for this dry wooden bench

to open, let you in, hear the stream
stones hear when young, not yet
sent to the bottom even in the afternoon.

\*

You dead still look out at water
are sheltered inside these row houses
laid down along the shore—each grave

SIMON PERCHIK

waiting for your Moses-like wave
the way a valley is dried
for rafts made from stone

though water never leaves you
covers each afternoon
with the few hours it needs

between your hands
kept separate to clear a path
as if nothing happened.

                              *

You squint as if its cries could fit,
and in the same pot this egg
lowered to the bottom—each wave

learns from the others just how much
end-over-end heats an inside
that has no shell, becomes a sea

overflows the way you dead are buried
embraced by a room filled with water
by walls built from wood and knots

and nails, has a door that opens up
whitewashed, sent out as daylight
all the time adding shoreline and salt.

SIMON PERCHIK

# SIT-UPON

ALYSE BENSEL

I wove yesterday's news for comfort.
Played kick-the-can ice cream, still mostly
cream by the end. Greedy for mountain
pies crammed with tomato sauce and melted
cheese from the campfire forge. Resisted
scraping the rare water penny from under
stream rocks, while the Boy Scouts netted
crayfish. Eating the torso, they squeezed off
the heads like bottle rockets. Too busy daring
another girl to eat burnt marshmallows
whole. Perpetual damp feasts for mildew.
Red rover. Bloody Mary. Mornings with dewy
eyelashes, a sleeping beauty no one would kiss.
Thinking I was dessert, I took care of that
myself, early and too sweet and awake.

# CONTRIBUTORS' NOTES

CONTRIBUTORS' NOTES

**Aholaah Arzah** received her MFA in Creative Writing from Goddard College. Her poems, essays, short fiction, and visuals have appeared in a variety of publications, including *Short, Fast and Deadly*, *Crab Creek Review*, and *Bellingham Review*. Her essay "Ring Cycle" received *Longshot Magazine*'s feature award.

**Melissa Atkinson Mercer** is the author of the poetry collections *Saint of the Partial Apology* (Five Oaks Press, 2017) and *Knock* (Half Mystic Press, forthcoming), as well as five chapbooks. Her work has recently appeared or is forthcoming in *Tinderbox Poetry Journal*, *Zone 3*, *Bone Bouquet*, and *A Portrait in Blues: An Anthology of Identity, Gender, and Bodies* (Platypus Press, 2017). She has an MFA from West Virginia University and currently works and teaches at Lees-McRae College.

**Walter Bargen** has published twenty books of poetry. Recent books include *Days Like This Are Necessary: New & Selected Poems* (BkMk Press, 2009), *Trouble Behind Glass Doors* (BkMk Press, 2013), and *Too Quick for the Living* (Moon City Press, 2017). His awards include a National Endowment for the Arts Fellowship and the William Rockhill Nelson Award. He was appointed the first Poet Laureate of Missouri (2008-2009). He can be found online at walterbargen.com.

**Adrianne Beer** is a recent graduate of Bowling Green State University, where she received a BFA in creative writing and a BA in communication. She currently lives in Chicago and works as an

AmeriCorps VISTA at Illinois Campus Compact. She is originally from Yellow Springs, Ohio.

**Alyse Bensel**'s poems have most recently appeared or are forthcoming in *The Adroit Journal, Tinderbox Poetry Journal, Quarterly West, New South*, and elsewhere. She is the author of the poetry chapbooks *Not of Their Own Making* (dancing girl press, 2014) and *Shift* (Plan B Press, 2012) and serves as book reviews editor at *The Los Angeles Review*. A doctoral candidate in creative writing at the University of Kansas, she lives in Lawrence.

**Roy Bentley** is the recipient of a Creative Writing Fellowship in poetry from the National Endowment for the Arts, as well as fellowships from Florida's Division of Cultural Affairs and the Ohio Arts Council. Books include *Boy in a Boat* (University of Alabama Press, 1986), *Any One Man* (Bottom Dog Press, 1992), *The Trouble with a Short Horse in Montana* (White Pine Press, 2006), *Starlight Taxi* (Lynx House Press, 2013), and *Walking with Eve in the Loved City*, a finalist for the Miller Williams Poetry Prize, due this year from the University of Arkansas Press.

**Melissa Boston**'s work also appears in *Midwestern Gothic, Bird's Thumb, I-70 Review, poemmemoirstory*, and others. She currently lives in Fayetteville, Arkansas.

**Jo Brachman**'s poems appear in *Best New Poets 2016, Cimarron Review, Bellingham Review, Poet Lore, Birmingham Poetry Review*, and many other journals. She is a fellow of the Hambidge Center for the Creative Arts and Sciences and the recipient of the 2017 Pine Lake MAPMAKERS Grant for poetry. She attends the MFA program at Pacific University in Portland, Oregon, and lives in the Atlanta area.

**Jennifer Bullis** is the author of the chapbook *Impossible Lessons* (MoonPath Press, 2013). Her poems and essays appear in *Gulf Coast, Tinderbox Poetry Journal, Water~Stone Review*, and *Nasty Women Poets: An Unapologetic Anthology of Subversive Verse* (Lost Horse Press, 2017). Her manuscript of resistance poems, *The Tongue of Narcissus*, is a finalist for the 2018 Brittingham and Pollak Poetry Prizes. Originally from

181

Reno, she earned a PhD in literature at the University of California, Davis. She lives in Bellingham, Washington, where she taught college writing and literature for fourteen years.

**Hisham Bustani** is a Jordanian author of five collections of short fiction and poetry. His book *The Perception of Meaning* (Syracuse University Press, 2015) won the 2014 University of Arkansas Arabic Translation Award. Most recently, one of his stories was featured in the inaugural edition of *The Best Asian Short Stories* anthology (Singapore: Kitaab, 2017).

**Astrid Cabral** is a leading poet and environmentalist from the Amazonian region of Brazil. She is the translator of Henry David Thoreau's *Walden* into Portuguese. Recent collections of her poetry include *The Anteroom* (2007), *Gazing Through Water* (2003), and *Cage* (Host Publications, 2008). Her poems have appeared in *Pleiades*, *The Cincinnati Review*, *The Evansville Review*, *Per Contra*, and elsewhere.

**Thomas Cardamone** is currently an MFA candidate in the Creative Writing Program at the University of Houston. His fiction has previously appeared in *Lunch Ticket*, *Necessary Fiction*, and *decomP*.

**Robin Cedar** earned her MFA in poetry from Oregon State University and served as poetry editor and social media manager for its literary journal, *45th Parallel*. Her work has been nominated for *Best of the Net* and has appeared in *Blue Mesa Review*, *Front Porch Journal*, *Pacifica Literary Review*, *LEVELER*, and elsewhere.

**Nick Christian**'s work has appeared or is forthcoming in *TAB*, *The Lindenwood Review*, *Cobalt*, *Rat's Ass Review*, and elsewhere.

**Clayton Adam Clark** lives in St. Louis, his hometown, where he works as a public health researcher and also volunteers as member of the board of directors for *River Styx*. His first full-length poetry collection, *A Finitude of Skin*, will be published by Moon City Press in November 2018. He earned an MFA in poetry at Ohio State University and is currently studying to become a clinical mental health counselor.

**Charlotte Covey** is from St. Mary's County, Maryland. Currently, she is an MFA candidate in poetry at the University of Missouri-St. Louis. She has poetry published or forthcoming in journals such as *The Normal School*, *Salamander*, *CALYX*, and *the minnesota review*, among others. In 2017, she was twice nominated for a Pushcart Prize. She is co-editor-in-chief of *Milk Journal* and an assistant editor of *Natural Bridge*.

**Debra Kang Dean** is the author of *Fugitive Blues* (Moon City Press, 2014), which won the Blue Moon Chapbook Contest in 2013. *Totem: America*, her third book of poetry, is forthcoming from Tiger Bark Press in 2018. Her poems have appeared in many journals, including, most recently, *The Hampden-Sydney Poetry Review*'s special issue on the sonnet. She teaches in Spalding University's low-residency MFA in Writing Program.

**Shelby Dale DeWeese** is an MFA candidate at the University of San Francisco, and her poems have appeared in such publications as *Rust + Moth*, *Quaint Magazine*, and *Marathon Literary Review*. Visit her online at shelbydaledeweese.com.

**Susan Frith** lives in Orlando, Florida, with her husband and two daughters. Her short fiction has appeared in *Nashville Review*, *New Madrid*, *Phoebe*, *Sycamore Review*, and other publications. She is working on a novel.

**Lukas Ray Hall** holds an MFA from Pacific University. His poems have appeared or are forthcoming in *Atlanta Review*, *The Florida Review*, *Midway Journal*, and *the minnesota review*, among other journals.

**Eileen Hennessy**'s work has appeared or is forthcoming in numerous literary magazines, including *The Paris Review*, *Western Humanities Review*, *Prairie Schooner*, *Whiskey Island Magazine*, and in several anthologies. Her poetry collection, *This Country of Gale-force Winds*, was published by New York Quarterly Books in 2011. Her second collection, *Places Where We Have Lived Forever*, was published in 2015 by Off The Park Press.

**Brandon Henry** is from Springfield, Missouri, returning in 2008 after living in Colorado. In a previous life, he worked in finance for ten years.

**Emma Johnson-Rivard** is a master's student at Hamline University. She received her undergraduate degree in film studies from Smith College in Massachusetts and currently lives in Minnesota with her dogs and far too many books. Her work has appeared in *Mistake House*, *Nixes Mate Review*, and *Santa Ana River Review*.

**Rosalind Kaliden** published her first chapbook, *Arriving Sideways*, with John Gosslee Books in 2016. Her poetry and essays have appeared in *Dappled Things*, *Fjords Review*, and the anthology *The Widows' Handbook* (Kent State University Press, 2014).

**Karla Keffer** is a doctoral candidate in English with an emphasis on creative writing/fiction at the University of Southern Mississippi, where she publishes the magazine *The Real Ramona*. Her poetry has been published in *Smartish Pace*.

**Ron Koertge** is the author of many novels, including *Stoner & Spaz* (Candlewick, 2011), *Strays* (Candlewick, 2010), and *The Brimstone Journals* (Candlewick, 2004), all American Library Association Best Books for Young Adults; *Shakespeare Bats Cleanup* (Candlewick, 2006), an American Library Association Top Ten Sports Books for Youth Selection; and *The Arizona Kid* (Candlewick, 2005), an American Library Association pick for "one of the ten funniest books of the year." A two-time winner of the PEN America Literary Award for children's literature, Ron lives in South Pasadena, California.

**Clayton Krollman** is a junior double-major in English and education at the University of Maryland.

**Ted Lardner**'s work has recently appeared or is forthcoming in *DIAGRAM*, *Bird's Thumb*, *Gone Lawn*, and *Blue Fifth Review*. *We Practice for It* (Tupelo Press, 2014) was selected by Mark Doty as the winner of the Sunken Garden Poetry Award.

184

**Gary Leising**'s books and chapbooks include *The Alp at the End of My Street* (Brick Road Poetry Press, 2014) and *Temple of Bones* (Finishing Line Press, 2013).

**Danèlle Lejeune** has published a full-length collection of poetry, *Landlocked: Etymology of Whale-Fish and Grace* (Finishing Line Press, 2017). Her poetry has also appeared or is forthcoming in *Whale Road Review*, *Glass: A Journal of Poetry*, *The Nottingham Review*, *Driftwood Poetry Journal*, and elsewhere.

**Saul Lemerond** is a third-year doctoral student at the University of Louisiana at Lafayette. His book, *Kayfabe & Other Stories*, was published by One Wet Shoe Publishing in 2013. His poetry, nonfiction, and short stories have also been published in *The Dunesteef Audio Fiction Magazine*, *The Drabblecast*, *Notes Magazine*, and elsewhere. He was a finalist for *The Conium Review*'s Innovative Short Fiction Contest and *Gigantic Sequins*'s Flash Fiction Contest.

**Alexis Levitin**'s forty books of translation include Clarice Lispector's *Soulstorm* (1989) and Eugenio de Andrade's *Forbidden Words* (2003), both from New Directions. Recent books include Santiago Vizcaino's *Destruction in the Afternoon* (Diálogos Books, 2015), Sophia de Mello Breyner Andresen's *Exemplary Tales* (Tagus Press, 2015) Salgado Maranhão's *Tiger Fur* (White Pine Press, 2015), and Rosa Alice Branco's *Cattle of the Lord* (Milkweed Editions, 2016).

**George Looney**'s recent books include *Meditations Before the Windows Fail* (Lost Horse Press, 2015), the book-length poem *Structures the Wind Sings Through* (Full/Crescent Press, 2014), *Monks Beginning to Waltz* (Truman State University Press, 2012), and *A Short Bestiary of Love and Madness* (Stephen F. Austin University Press, 2011). His novel *Report from a Place of Burning* will be published in fall of 2018 by Leapfrog Press. He founded the BFA in Creative Writing Program at Penn State Erie, where he is distinguished professor of literature and creative writing and editor of the international literary journal *Lake Effect*.

**Naomi Ruth Lowinsky** won the 2014 Blue Light Poetry Prize for her chapbook, *The Little House on Stilts Remembers* (Blue Light Press, 2015). Her fourth full-length collection, *The Faust Woman Poems* (il piccolo editions, 2013). A new collection of essays, *The Rabbi, The Goddess, and Jung: Getting the Word from Within*, was published by Fisher King Press in 2016. She is a Jungian analyst and blogs about poetry and life at sisterfrombelow.com.

**Wyatt McMurry** is an MFA candidate in poetry at the University of Alabama.

**Michael Meyerhofer**'s fifth poetry book, *Ragged Eden*, is forthcoming from Glass Lyre Press. His work has appeared in *Ploughshares*, *Rattle*, *Hayden's Ferry Review*, *Mid-American Review*, and other journals. He is also the author of a fantasy series and serves as poetry editor for *Atticus Review*. For more info, visit troublewithhammers.com.

**Emily O'Neill** teaches writing and tends bar in Boston. Her debut poetry collection, *Pelican*, was the inaugural winner of YesYes Books' Pamet River Prize for women and non-binary writers in 2015 and the winner of the 2016 Devil's Kitchen Reading Award. Her second collection, *a falling knife has no handle*, is forthcoming from YesYes Books in 2018. She is the author of three chapbooks, and her recent work has appeared in *CutBank*, *Redivider*, *Salt Hill*, and *Washington Square Review*.

**Wendy Oleson** is the author of *Please Find Us*, winner of Gertrude Press' 2017 Fiction Chapbook Contest, and *Our Daughter and Other Stories* (2017), winner of *Map Literary*'s 2016 Rachel Wetzsteon Chapbook Award. Her stories and hybrid work have recently appeared in *Cimarron Review*, *Copper Nickel*, and *Crab Orchard Review*. She teaches for the Writers' Program at UCLA Extension and at Washington State University Tri-Cities, and she serves as associate prose editor for *Fairy Tale Review* and as assistant fiction editor for *Memorious*.

**Aza Pace**'s poems have appeared or are forthcoming in *The Southern Review*, *The Madison Review*, *Common Ground Review*, and *The*

*Harpoon Review*, among others. She is the winner of a 2017 Inprint Donald Barthelme Prize in Poetry, and her work has been nominated for a Pushcart Prize and for *Best New Poets*.

**Ricardo Pau-Llosa**'s eighth book of poetry is due out next year from Carnegie Mellon University Press, publisher of his previous five titles. Recent and forthcoming poetry publicatioins include *New England Review*, *Boston Review*, *Colorado Review*, and *Virginia Quarterly Review*.

**Simon Perchik** is an attorney whose poems have appeared in *Partisan Review, Forge, Poetry, Osiris, The New Yorker* and elsewhere. His most recent collection is *The Osiris Poems*, published by boxofchalk in 2017. Visit his website, simonperchik.com.

**Lizzy Petersen** is a St. Louis native. Her poetry has appeared or is forthcoming in *Apalachee Review, Birmingham Poetry Review, The Journal,* and *New South*. Her poetry reviews have appeared in *Coldfront, Poetry Magazine*'s *Harriet* blog, and the *St. Louis Post-Dispatch*.

**Leslie Pietrzyk** is the author of *Pears on a Willow Tree* (Harper Perennial, 1999) and *A Year and a Day* (William Morrow, 2004), both novels. Her collection of unconventionally linked short stories, *This Angel on My Chest*, won the 2015 Drue Heinz Literature Prize and was published by the University of Pittsburgh Press in 2017. A new novel, *Silver Girl*, will be published by the Unnamed Press in February 2018. Her short fiction and essays have appeared or are forthcoming in *The Southern Review, The Gettysburg Review, The Sun, River Styx*, and many other journals. She is a member of the core fiction faculty for Converse College's low-residency MFA program. She lives in Alexandria, Virginia.

**Elizabeth Rees** is the author of *Every Root a Branch* (Codhill Press, 2014) and three chapbooks. Twice nominated for a Pushcart Prize, her work has been widely published, including in *AGNI, The Southern Review,* and *Kenyon Review*. She teaches poetry writing to children and adults in the DC Metro Area.

187

**henry 7. reneau, jr.,** is the author of the poetry collection *freedomland blues* (Transcendent Zero Press, 2015) and the e-chapbook *physiography of the fittest* (Kind of a Hurricane Press, 2014). Additionally, he has self-published a chapbook entitled *13hirteen Levels of Resistance* and is currently working on a book of connected short stories.

**Ron Riekki**'s books include *U.P.* (Ghost Road Press, 2008), *The Way North: Collected Upper Peninsula New Works* (Wayne State University Press, 2013), and *Here: Women Writing on Michigan's Upper Peninsula* (Michigan State University Press, 2015).

**Jacki Rigoni** writes and teaches within the found spaces of single-parenting her three children in the San Francisco Bay Area. She has an MA in English from the University of California, Berkeley. She was a finalist for the 2018 Francine Ringold Award for New Writers, and her poems are forthcoming in *Nimrod International Journal* and *Poems-For-All*. She writes on her site, WomanUprising.com.

**A.R. Robins** is pursuing her master's degree at Southeast Missouri State University. Her fiction has been featured on the podcast *Second Hand Stories*. Her poetry and fiction have been published or are forthcoming in *The Cape Rock*, *Atlas & Alice*, *The Swamp*, *Foliate Oak Literary Magazine*, and other journals.

**Gage Saylor** is a writer, editor, and actor from Charleston, South Carolina. His work has appeared in *BULL* and *TINGE Magazine*. He was fiction editor for the most recent issue of *The McNeese Review* and is currently finishing his MFA at McNeese State University. He has also appeared on the Emmy-winning television series *The Inspectors*.

**Breea Schutt** has always had a God-given passion for storytelling. After graduating with her MA in creative writing, she hopes to continue teaching fiction classes and find an agent to represent her finished manuscript.

**Lucas Southworth**'s stories are forthcoming or have recently appeared in *AGNI*, *Alaska Quarterly Review*, *Web Conjunctions*, *Willow*

*Springs,* and other journals. His collection of short stories, *Everyone Here Has a Gun,* won AWP's Grace Paley Prize (University of Massachusetts Press, 2013). He lives in Baltimore, where he teaches writing at Loyola University Maryland.

**Joshua Michael Stewart** has had poems published in *The Massachusetts Review, Rattle, Atticus Review, Brilliant Corners,* and many other journals. His collection of poems, *Break Every String,* was published by Hedgerow Books in 2016. Visit him online at joshuamichaelstewart.com.

Born in Lebanon, **maia tabet** is a literary translator and a professional cook now living in the United States. She is the translator of Elias Khoury's first novel to be published in English, *Little Mountain* (Picador, 2007), and of *White Masks* (Archipelago, 2010). She has also translated excerpts of poetry by the Syrian poet Adonis.

**Jason Teal** is a writer now living in Manhattan, Kansas. He runs *Heavy Feather Review* and organizes readings at Arrow Coffee Company. His work appears in *Knee-Jerk, SmokeLong Quarterly, Hobart,* and *Quarterly West,* among other publications.

**Mary Troy** is the author of the novels *Swimming on Hwy N* (Moon City Press, 2016) and *Beauties* (BkMk Press, 2010), winner of the USA Book Award and a finalist for a Foreword INDIES Book of the Year Award. She is also the author of three collections of short stories: *Cookie Lily* (Southern Methodist University Press, 2004), *The Alibi Cafe and Other Stories* (BkMk Press, 2003), and *Joe Baker Is Dead* (University of Missouri Press, 1998). She teaches fiction writing and contemporary literature for the University of Missouri-St. Louis and is Editor of *Natural Bridge.*

**Barbara Varanka** lives and works in Kansas City, Missouri. She holds an MFA in Creative Writing and Media Arts from the University of Missouri-Kansas City and has been published in journals such as *Bear Review, Jet Fuel Review,* and *Booth.*

**Giovanna Varela**'s work is severely influenced by her home region of Central Florida. She is pursuing an MFA in creative writing at The New School and an MFA in film production at Emerson College. She is the winner of *Big Muddy*'s 2017 Mighty River Short Story Contest, and her pilot script *Flamingo City* earned second place in the Nevada International Film Festival's 2017 Best TV Screenplay competition. Her flash fiction has been published in *FOLIO*, *Literary Juice*, *Rock & Sling*, and *Southern Indiana Review*.

**Charles Harper Webb**'s latest collection of poems, *Sidebend World*, will be published by the University of Pittsburgh Press in 2018. *A Million MFAs Are Not Enough*, a gathering of Webb's essays on contemporary American poetry, was published in 2016 by Red Hen Press. A recipient of grants from the Whiting and Guggenheim Foundations, Webb teaches creative writing at California State University, Long Beach.

**Gabriel Welsch** is the author of four poetry collections, the most recent being *The Four Horsepersons of a Disappointing Apocalypse* (Steel Toe Books, 2013). His fiction and poetry have appeared in journals including *The Georgia Review*, *The Southern Review*, *Harvard Review*, and *The Missouri Review*, as well as on *Verse Daily* and in Ted Kooser's column *American Life in Poetry*. He lives in Huntingdon, Pennsylvania, with his family, works as vice president of Strategic Communication and marketing at Juniata College, and is an occasional teacher at the Chautauqua Writer's Center.

**Lesley Wheeler**'s chapbook *Propagation* is just out from dancing girl press. She is the author of several collections, including *Radioland* (2015) and *Heterotopia* (2010), both from Barrow Street Press. She blogs about poetry at http://lesleywheeler.org/ and teaches at Washington and Lee University in Lexington, Virginia.

**William Woolfitt** is the author of three poetry collections: *Beauty Strip* (Texas Review Press, 2015), *Charles of the Desert* (Paraclete Press, 2016), and *Spring Up Everlasting* (Paraclete Press,

forthcoming). His poems, short stories, and essays have appeared or are forthcoming in *Tin House*, *The Threepenny Review*, *AGNI*, and *The Gettysburg Review*, among other journals.

**Kirby Wright** won the award for the best screenplay at the 2018 Caribbean Sea International Film Festival. His latest book is *At the Customs House* (2017), a collection of poetry and flash fiction set in Helsinki and Stockholm.

191